NAT
CHINA
O.
EXCHANGES

家博物馆
流系列丛书

美的多元

古希腊的艺术与生活

高政 主编
Gao Zheng　Chief Editor for the Series

THE COUNTLESS ASPECTS OF
BEAUTY IN ANCIENT ART

From the Collections of
the Hellenic National Archaeological Museum

中国国家博物馆
NATIONAL MUSEUM OF CHINA

HELLENIC REPUBLIC
Ministry of Culture

ΕΘΝΙΚΟ ΑΡΧΑΙΟΛΟΓΙΚΟ ΜΟΥΣΕΙΟ
HELLENIC NATIONAL ARCHAEOLOGICAL MUSEUM

中国出版集团
中译出版社
China Publishing Group
China Translation and Publishing House

图书在版编目（CIP）数据

美的多元：古希腊的艺术与生活：汉英对照 / 高
政主编. -- 北京：中译出版社，2024. 11（2025.5重印）.
-- ISBN 978-7-5001-8101-9

Ⅰ. K885.45

中国国家版本馆CIP数据核字第2024KZ1845号

美的多元：古希腊的艺术与生活
MEI DE DUOYUAN: GUXILA DE YISHU YU SHENGHUO

出版发行　中译出版社
地　　址　北京市西城区新街口外大街28号普天德胜大厦主楼4层
电　　话　（010）68359373，68359827（发行部）68357328（编辑部）
邮　　编　100088
电子邮箱　book@ctph.com.cn
网　　址　http://www.ctph.com.cn

总 策 划　刘永淳
策划编辑　赵　青
责任编辑　范　伟　马雨晨
文字编辑　赵　青　马雨晨　朱安琪
专家审核　王以欣　张新刚
外语校译　曹秀媛　王广州　郑惠中
封面设计　上官天梦

排　　版　上官天梦
印　　刷　北京雅昌艺术印刷有限公司
经　　销　新华书店

规　　格　235毫米 × 305毫米　1/8
印　　张　33.25
字　　数　201千字
版　　次　2024年11月第1版
印　　次　2025年5月第2次印刷

ISBN　978-7-5001-8101-9　　定价：469.00元

The exhibition "The Countless Aspects of Beauty in Ancient Art" is an exclusive creation and production of the Hellenic National Archaeological Museum, owing its concept, museological development and curation to Dr. Maria Lagogianni-Georgakarakos, Director Emerita of the Hellenic National Archaeological Museum and Vice President of the Board of the Hellenic National Archaeological Museum.

An integral part of the exhibition is the Greek and English edition of the scientific catalogue, under the general supervision of Dr. Maria Lagogianni-Georgakarakos, which accompanied the exhibition during its presentation at the National Archaeological Museum in 2018, with the following bibliographic reference: Maria Lagogianni-Georgakarakos (ed.), *The Countless Aspects of Beauty in Ancient Art*, Exhibition Catalogue, Athens 2018 (publ. HOCRD).

The present catalogue of Greek antiquities presented in the current homonymous exhibition is the result of a collaboration between the Hellenic National Archaeological Museum and the National Museum of China.

The entries and short texts in this catalogue derive from the accompanying exhibition texts.

中国国家博物馆
NATIONAL MUSEUM OF CHINA

HELLENIC REPUBLIC
Ministry of Culture

ΕΘΝΙΚΟ ΑΡΧΑΙΟΛΟΓΙΚΟ ΜΟΥΣΕΙΟ
HELLENIC NATIONAL ARCHAEOLOGICAL MUSEUM

希腊方图录项目组
CATALOGUE EDITORIAL TEAM OF
THE HELLENIC NATIONAL ARCHAEOLOGICAL MUSEUM

SPECIAL CHIEF EDITOR

Dr. Anna Vasiliki Karapanagiotou

AUTHORS

Sapfo Athanasopoulou (MA)

Dr. Christina Avronidaki

Alexandra Chatzipanagiotou (MA)

Dr. Maria Chidiroglou

Dr. Despoina Ignatiadou

Dr. Despoina Kalessopoulou

Dr. Giorgos Kavvadias

Dr. Eleni Konstantinidi-Syvridi

Dr. Katerina Kostanti

Panagiota Koutsiana

Dr. Evrydiki Leka

Dr. Katia Manteli

Dr. Kostas Nikolentzos

Dr. Efi Oikonomou

Dr. Kostas Paschalidis

Dr. Vassiliki Pliatsika

Dr. Maria Salta

Dr. Maria Selekou

Dr. Chrysanthi Tsouli

Dr. Elena Vlachogianni

Dr. Katerina Voutsa

EDITORIAL COMMUNICATION

Maria Terzoudi (MSc)

PHOTOGRAPHS

Photographic Archive of the Hellenic

National Archaeological Museum

Eleftherios A. Galanopoulos

Kiki Birtacha

Giorgos Fafalis

Pantelis Feleris

Hans Rupprecht Goette

Ilias Iliadis

Georgia Karamargiou

Maria Kontaki

Panayotis Lazaris

Despoina Marsinopoulou

Sokratis Mavrommatis

Eirini Miari

Ioannis Panagakos

Yannis Patrikianos

Spilios Pistas

Stelios Skourlis

Despoina Spyrou

Stefanos Stournaras

Kalliopi Tsakri

Tassos Vrettos

Kostas Xenikakis

中国国家博物馆策展团队
EXHIBITION TEAM OF
THE NATIONAL MUSEUM OF CHINA

学术顾问 / Academic Advisor

陈煜 Chen Yu

丁宁 Ding Ning

晏绍祥 Yan Shaoxiang

策展人 / Curator

朱晓云 Zhu Xiaoyun

策展助理 / Curatorial Assistant

孟岩 Meng Yan

张艺帆 Zhang Yifan

内容设计 / Content Design

张艺帆 Zhang Yifan

朱晓云 Zhu Xiaoyun

空间设计 / Interior Design

邓璐 Deng Lu

刘蔚娴 Liu Weixian

平面设计 / Graphic Design

上官天梦 Shangguan Tianmeng

连洁茜 Lian Jiexi

展品点交 / Condition Check

马立治 Ma Lizhi

王志强 Wang Zhiqiang

贾树 Jia Shu

许梦颖 Xu Mengying

张鹏宇 Zhang Pengyu

雷磊 Lei Lei

晏德付 Yan Defu

李沫 Li Mo

徐强 Xu Qiang

董梅 Dong Mei

吕东莹 Lyu Dongying

李瑶 Li Yao

赵子琪 Zhao Ziqi

王一铭 Wang Yiming

国际协调 / International Coordination

张艺帆 Zhang Yifan

数据保障 / Data Support

周子杰 Zhou Zijie

新闻传播 / Press Office

王扬 Wang Yang

社会教育 / Public Education

戴萌 Dai Meng

行政协调 / Administrative Support

李静 Li Jing

法务支持 / Legal Support

李铁飞 Li Tiefei

翻译审核 / Proofreading

何书铱 He Shuyi

王一铭 Wang Yiming

董梅 Dong Mei

财务管理 / Finance and Auditing

龚志陆 Gong Zhilu

安全保障 / Safety and Security

白晨明 Bai Chenming

赵泽 Zhao Ze

设备保障 / Facilities

陈晨 Chen Chen

高阳 Gao Yang

李艳龙 Li Yanlong

后勤保障 / Logistics

郭婧 Guo Jing

布展协调 / Exhibition Coordination

王沛然 Wang Peiran

陈凯 Chen Kai

文物加固 / Mount Support

廉成海 Lian Chenghai

王浩 Wang Hao

蔡利涛 Cai Litao

付志银 Fu Zhiyin

文创开发 / Merchandising

廖飞 Liao Fei

郑中允子 Zheng Zhongyunzi

文字编辑 / Text Support

张雪嫣 Zhang Xueyan

地图协助 / Map Support

韩旭川 Han Xuchuan

ORIGIN OF EXHIBITS

Hellenic National Archaeological Museum

IDEA - CONCEPT- MUSEOLOGICAL DEVELOPMENT

Dr. Maria Lagogianni-Georgakarakos
Archaeologist, Director Emerita of the National Archaeological Museum, Vice President of the Board of the Hellenic National Archaeological Museum

GENERAL COORDINATION

Dr. Anna Vasiliki Karapanagiotou, Director General of the Hellenic National Archaeological Museum

PROJECT MANAGEMENT - TECHNICAL SUPERVISION

Kelly Drakomathioulaki, Deputy Head of the Department of Technical Support and Museography

ARCHAEOLOGICAL SUPERVISION

Dr. Despoina Ignatiadou, Head of the Department of Sculpture Collection
Dr. George Kavvadias, Head of the Department of Vases, Metalwork and Minor Art Collections
Dr. Konstantinos Nikolentzos, Head of the Department of Collections of Prehistoric, Egyptian, Cypriot and Near Eastern Antiquities

CONSERVATION SUPERVISION

Dr. Georgianna Moraitou, Head of the Department of Conservation, Physical and Chemical Research and Archaeometry

COMMUNICATION SUPERVISION

Dr. Evangelos Vivliodetis, Head of the Department of Exhibitions, Communication and Education
Kelly Drakomathioulaki, Deputy Head of the Department of Technical Support and Museography

WORKING GROUP - CURATION

Kelly Drakomathioulaki, Civil Engineer, Deputy Head of the Department of Technical Support and Museography
Sapfo Athanasopoulou, Archaeologist, (MA) Museum Studies, Department of Vases, Metalwork and Minor Art Collections.
Panagiotis Lazaris, Conservator, (MA) Conservation of Historic Objects, Department of Conservation, Physical and Chemical Research and Archaeometry
Dr. Efi Oikonomou, Archaeologist, Department of Vases, Metalwork and Minor Art Collections
Dr. Vassiliki Pliatsika, Archaeologist, Department of Collections of Prehistoric, Egyptian, Cypriot and Near Eastern Antiquities
Maria Terzoudi, Archaeologist, (MSc) Cultural Management, Department of Exhibitions, Communication and Education
Kalliopi Tsakri, Conservator, (MSc) Conservation Science, Department of Conservation, Physical and Chemical Research and Archaeometry

Dr. Chrysanthi Tsouli, Archaeologist, Department of Sculpture Collection
Dr. Katerina Voutsa, Archaeologist, Department of Collections of Prehistoric, Egyptian, Cypriot and Near Eastern Antiquities

CONSERVATION OF EXHIBITS

Department of Conservation, Physical-Chemical Research and Archaeometry
Conservators of Antiquities
Panagiotis Athanasopoulos, Georgia Karamargiou, Maria Kontaki, Panagiotis Lazaris, Despoina Marsinopoulou, Ioannis Panagakos, Kalliopi Tsakri, Katerina Xylina

INSTALLATION OF EXHIBITS

Georgia Karamargiou, Panagiotis Lazaris, Despoina Marsinopoulou, Ioannis Panagakos, Kalliopi Tsakri

MUSIC

Nina, Pinta, Santa Maria ("1492 - Conquest of Paradise"), by Vangelis Papathanasiou (Vangelis) (late composer V. Papathanasiou royalties manager)
"9 Muses", by Nikolaos Xanthoulis (courtesy of the composer)

DIGITAL APPLICATIONS-VIDEOS-3D DIGITAL IMAGING
HELLENIC NATIONAL ARCHAEOLOGICAL MUSEUM
PRODUCTION

Section 2 "The Beautiful and the Desirable":
Restoring Beauty: Ioannis Panagakos (MA) Digital Arts, Kalliopi Tsakri
Ingredients of perfume oils from Linear B tablets: Pantelis Feleris
Section 3 "Focusing on the Body":
Rendering the human body in the passage of time: Ioannis Panagakos, Kalliopi Tsakri
Section 4 "Epilogue: Endless Quest":
The Countless aspects of Beauty: Maria Lagogianni- Georgakarakos, Photis Papatheodorou

Video

"A jewel made in Greece" by the homonymous platform, with the contribution of the HNAM and the kind participation of Ms. Katerina Didaskalou, actress.

COORDINATION ON BEHALF OF THE HELLENIC MINISTRY OF CULTURE

Directorate General of Antiquities and Cultural Heritage
Dr. Olympia Vikatou, Director General

Directorate of Archaeological Museums, Exhibitions and Educational Programs
Nikoletta Saraga, Archaeologist (MA), Deputy Director
Christos Koutsothanasis, Archaeologist – Museologist (MSc)

致　辞

希腊文化部 部长
莉娜·门佐尼博士

近年来，希腊与中国合作持续加强，在多个领域取得了快速发展。其中，文化交流与合作尤为突出，意义重大且发展前景广阔。希腊与中国均以悠久的历史而闻名，两国都致力于文化遗产的保存、保护和弘扬，视其为未来繁荣与发展的宝贵资源。

作为2021"中国希腊文化和旅游年"的一部分，也为了响应中国民众对希腊文化日益高涨的热情，希腊原计划将有一系列大型展览在中国多家知名博物馆巡回展出。然而，突如其来的新冠疫情导致原定的展览计划不得不推迟和改期。本次"美的多元——古希腊的艺术与生活"展原计划于2020年在中国国家博物馆举办。随着导致该展览推迟的各种原因已离我们远去，2024年11月至2025年6月，希腊文化部终于可以自豪地向中国公众推出本次展览。

"美的多元——古希腊的艺术与生活"展最初于2018年至2019年由希腊国家考古博物馆为庆祝其建馆150周年而举办，并巡展至希腊其他博物馆。展出期间，希腊和外国媒体将其誉为重要的文化里程碑，追溯了古希腊从新石器时代到古典晚期对美的不懈追求。在此基础上，我们进行了略微的修改和删减，本次展览共包括279件原件、铸件、数字展品，以及希腊著名音乐家范吉利斯·帕帕坦纳西乌和尼科斯·桑图利斯的音乐作品，邀请中国观众探索古希腊艺术和文化中永恒的美学概念。

纵观人类历史，"美"这一普世主题不断影响着文明和文化的表现形式。在古希腊，美不仅是一种审美理想，也是日常生活、哲学和艺术的核心主题。正如本次展览所示，美是一个多元、普遍和不断发展的概念，在大自然中、在日常用品工艺中、在不朽的艺术和建筑作品中随处可见。美源于感官的愉悦，同时反映了更深层的文化、社会和政治观念。古希腊人认为，美不仅是对人类形体的反映，也是身体与心灵之间的和谐平衡。柏拉图和亚里士多德等哲学家将美的本质视为一种道德和智慧的卓越形式，与真理和美德密切相关。本次精心挑选的展品旨在展示这些理想观念，每件展品都揭示了希腊古代社会如何从外在形态和概念深度两方面以艺术来表现美。

希腊国家考古博物馆和中国国家博物馆通过携手合作本次展览，为公众提供了一个难得的机会，可以欣赏和感受至今仍影响着整个世界的厚重的美学遗产。此次展览的终极目的，不仅是展示古希腊的辉煌成就，更是通过呈现超越文化和时代界限的人类对美的共同追求，促进东西方之间的对话与交流，为不同民族和传统文化之间搭建起沟通的桥梁。随着展览在北京展出，它将继续激发我们对美的多样性的思考，以及对美是如何影响我们对艺术、文化和身份的理解。我们诚挚地邀请中国朋友来探索这些精美的展品及其展示的观念和经验，并思考和分享自己对美的感悟。

我谨向中国政府和中国国家博物馆致以最诚挚的感谢，为我们提供了与中国公众近距离接触的宝贵机会，以及他们对希腊文化瑰宝的热情欢迎和接待。同时，我还要感谢希腊国家考古博物馆的工作人员及馆长安娜－瓦西莉基·卡拉帕纳约杜博士，以及为本次展览组织和图录出版做出贡献的所有人士，正是他们的专业知识和辛勤努力保证了本次展览的成功举办。

GREETINGS

Hellenic Ministry of Culture, Minister

Dr. Lina Mendoni

In recent years, the enduring relationship between Greece and China has not only strengthened but also progressed rapidly across multiple sectors. Among these, cultural exchange and cooperation stand out as areas of significant and promising development. Both Greeks and Chinese are celebrated for their rich, ancient histories, and they share a deep commitment to preserving, protecting, and promoting their cultural heritage—viewing it as a vital asset for future prosperity and growth.

As part of the "Greece-China Year of Culture and Tourism 2021" and in response to the growing enthusiasm among the Chinese people to explore key aspects of Greek culture, a series of major traveling exhibitions was planned to be showcased at several prominent museums across China. However, the onset of the COVID-19 pandemic caused considerable disruption, leading to their postponement and rescheduling. One such exhibition, titled "The Countless Aspects of Beauty in Ancient Art", was originally planned to take place at the National Museum of China in Beijing in 2020. With the adverse circumstances that delayed this project now behind us, the Hellenic Ministry of Culture is proud to finally present the exhibition to the Chinese public from November 2024 to June 2025.

The exhibition "The Countless Aspects of Beauty in Ancient Art" was initially organized and hosted by the National Archaeological Museum in Athens in 2018–2019 to mark its 150th anniversary. A traveling version was concurrently presented at other museums across Greece. At the time, the Greek and foreign media hailed it as a significant cultural milestone, tracing the ancient Greek pursuit of beauty from the Neolithic Age to Late Antiquity. In this new setting, a slightly revised and abridged version of the original exhibition—comprising 279 original works, one cast, digital exhibits, and the emblematic music of Vangelis Papathanassiou and Nikos Xanthoulis—invites Chinese audiences to explore the timeless concept of beauty as manifested in ancient Greek art and culture.

Throughout human history, the concept of beauty has been a universal concern, shaping civilizations and cultural expressions. In ancient Greece, beauty was not just an aesthetic ideal but a central theme of daily life, philosophy, and art. Beauty, as the exhibition demonstrates, is a multifaceted, universal, and evolving concept. It can be sought and found all around us—in nature, in the craftsmanship of simple everyday utilitarian objects, as well as in monumental works of art and architecture. While beauty is rooted in the pleasure of the senses, it also reflects deeper cultural, social, and political values. The ancient Greeks saw beauty not only as a reflection of the human form but also as a harmonious balance between the physical and the intellectual. Philosophers like Plato and Aristotle explored the nature of beauty as a form of moral and intellectual excellence, one that was intimately connected to truth and virtue. The selected exhibits aim to demonstrate these ideals, with each piece revealing how ancient societies used art to engage with beauty, both in its physical form and its conceptual depth.

The partnership between the Hellenic National Archaeological Museum in Athens and the National Museum of China in Beijing, within the context of this exhibition, offers a rare opportunity to engage with a profound legacy of beauty that continues to influence the entire world. The ultimate objective of this endeavor exceeds merely showcasing the achievements of ancient Greece; it seeks to encourage dialogue between East and West, bridging peoples and traditions by revealing the common and universal human pursuit of beauty, which transcends cultures and eras. As the exhibition embarks on its new journey in Beijing, it continues to inspire reflection on the countless aspects of beauty and the ways it shapes our understanding of art, culture, and human identity. We wholeheartedly invite our Chinese friends to explore this remarkable collection of objects, notions, and experiences, and to reflect on and share their own personal perceptions of beauty.

In offering us this tremendous opportunity to reach out to the Chinese public, as well as for their warm welcome and generous hospitality toward the Greek cultural treasures, I wish to express my deepest appreciation and gratitude to the Chinese authorities and the administrators of the emblematic National Museum of China. I also wish to thank the staff of the Hellenic National Archaeological Museum in Athens and its Director General, Dr. Anna Vasiliki Karapanagiotou, as well as the numerous contributors to the organization of this exhibition and the preparation of the accompanying catalog, whose expertise and arduous efforts were crucial for the successful outcome of this venture.

致　辞

希腊文化部 文化秘书长

乔治·迪达克拉罗杜博士

"美的多元——古希腊的艺术与生活"展是一场启迪心智的文化盛宴，深入挖掘了人类存在的核心价值、意义和美的本质。本次展览由希腊文化部及希腊国家考古博物馆精心策划，带领观众踏上穿越时空的美学之旅，追溯普遍存在而又千变万化的"美"的多重表现形式。

展览精选279件来自希腊各地的古代艺术品，时间脉络从新石器时代绵延至古典晚期，为观众呈现了一幅视觉与审美交织的宏伟画卷。

这些艺术品不仅见证了人类对美的不懈追求，更展示了美在历史长河中的多样风貌。在新石器时代迪米尼陶器的精美线性图案中，我们得以窥见美的初步显现；在早期基克拉迪文化的抽象大理石雕像中，我们感受到了美的深沉韵味；在色彩斑斓的锡拉岛与迈锡尼宫殿的遗迹中，我们体验到了美的绚烂多彩；而在古典时期希腊伟大艺术家的雕塑创作中，我们更是对美产生了无尽的赞叹。

博物馆采用独特的叙事手法，将美呈现为一种持续演变且永恒发展的真实存在。这一理念植根于古希腊哲学家赫拉克利特（约公元前535—前475）的思想，他提出世界处在永恒变化之中，和而不同。展览循序渐进地向现代观众揭示了审美观念历经世纪更迭的无数精彩演变。

古希腊人的审美偏好，借助其丰富多彩的神话传承、考古发现，以及古希腊哲学对身体之美、中庸之道和男子气概作为"善"和"美"的深刻阐释，得以生动展现。

在此，我谨向希腊国家考古博物馆和中国国家博物馆致以热烈的祝贺和诚挚的谢意。感谢双方以专业素养与创新精神，携手打造了这次非凡的博物馆之旅。

通过此类开创性的协作，文化的视野得以不断拓展。我衷心期待，这次精彩的展览能成为两国进一步深化文化合作的重要契机。

GREETINGS

Hellenic Ministry of Culture, Secretary General

Dr. Georgios Didaskalou

"The Countless Aspects of Beauty in Ancient Art" is an evocative and thought-provoking exhibition about human existence, exploring both the importance and the essence of its value and beauty. Designed by the Hellenic National Archaeological Museum of the Hellenic Ministry of Culture the exhibition takes visitors on a fascinating journey through time, tracing the universal and complex phenomenon of Beauty in all its forms.

The exhibition presents 279 selected ancient artworks that come from various regions of Greece and date from the Neolithic period to Late Antiquity, offering a feast of aesthetic gratifications.

The constant search for Beauty and the inexhaustible ways in which it has been presented aesthetically in the past can be seen in the impressive linear patterns of the Neolithic ceramics from Dimini, in the abstract marble figurines of the early Cycladic culture, in the colorful world of Thira and the Mycenaean palaces and in the admirable sculptural creations of the great Greek artists of classical times.

The museological narrative follows Beauty as a constantly evolving reality, gradually revealing to the eyes of the modern viewer countless versions of aesthetic unfolding over the centuries, in the worldview of Heraclitus (c. 535-475 BC), who spoke of the constant change of the world and the harmony of differences.

The aesthetic preferences of the ancient Greeks are revealed through their rich tradition of mythology, the archaeological finds, as well as how ancient Greek philosophy defined notions of physical beauty, moderation and manhood as the "Good" and the "Beautiful".

My deepest congratulations and sincere gratitude to the Hellenic National Archaeological Museum and the National Museum of China (NMC) for their expert collaboration and innovative partnership, which culminated in an extraordinary museum experience.

Through pioneering synergies, culture continues to expand its horizons. I wish that this remarkable exhibition will become an occasion for further cultural collaboration between our two countries.

致　　辞

希腊文化部 文物与文化遗产局局长

奥林匹娅·维卡图博士

希腊国家考古博物馆与中国国家博物馆联合举办的"美的多元——古希腊的艺术与生活"展为我们开辟了一条崭新的文化交流之路。展览如同一座文化桥梁，连接中希两国，再次彰显了希腊遗产的全球影响力与价值，展现了古希腊艺术在国际文化舞台上的恒久魅力。

展览以"美"与"美丽"为核心理念，引领观众穿越时空，从史前时代、米诺斯文明、基克拉迪文明、迈锡尼文明，直至古典主义的成熟，全方位展示了古希腊文化的美学成就。这些珍贵的艺术品，始终以人类为核心，深刻揭示了经济、社会与文化层面的丰富内涵。

作为希腊国家考古博物馆在中国的形象代表，本次展览为观众奉献了一场视觉盛宴，通过形式多样、内涵丰富的珍贵文物，充分展现了"美"与"美丽"的无穷魅力。这些瑰宝不仅令人叹为观止，更使人陶醉其中。它们以千变万化的形态与表现手法，深刻体现了人类对精神境界与审美创造的不懈追求。

希腊国家考古博物馆的展览理念是现代精神的杰出体现。作为文物与文化遗产局局长，我对此项目深表敬意，并衷心祝愿它在中国这一美丽的国度取得圆满成功，让古希腊人眼中的"美"，远离其存续千年的故土仍能璀璨绽放。

在此，我谨以希腊文化部文物与文化遗产局局长的身份，向所有支持展览组织工作，并为展览成功举办紧密合作的机构和人员表示衷心的感谢与热烈的祝贺。

新版图录将成为观众、研究人员和艺术爱好者的宝贵工具，助力他们在全球对话中拓宽"美"的视野，更深入地理解"美"的内涵与演变。

我期望这本图录能成为文化和科学界取之不尽、用之不竭的知识源泉，同时也成为深入思考与研究的基石。

最后，我衷心祝愿展览取得圆满成功，不仅将引发众多观众的强烈共鸣，更将为宣传与提升公众保护并传承文化遗产的意识作出重大贡献。

GREETINGS

Hellenic Ministry of Culture, Director General of Antiquities and Cultural Heritage

Dr. Olympia Vikatou

The Hellenic National Archaeological Museum's temporary exhibition titled "The Countless Aspects of Beauty in Ancient Art", presented at the National Museum of China (NMC) in Beijing, opens a new exhibition route and creates a cultural bridge between our countries, proving once again the global impact and value of the Greek heritage, as well as the continuing influence of the ancient Greek art on the international cultural scene.

The promotion of the ancient Greek culture through this exhibition and especially through the concept of Beauty and the "Beautiful" that traverses from the prehistoric era, the Minoan, the Cycladic and the Mycenaean world to the formation of the Classical Ideal, creates rules of high aesthetics, reflecting the economic, social and cultural dimension of art, keeping the human always in the center.

The current exhibition, as an ambassador in China of the Hellenic National Archaeological Museum, offers to the Chinese public treasures exhibited in the Greek museum and presents an extraordinary variety of manifestations of Beauty and the "Beautiful", which fascinate human thought, enchant the senses and define, through their constant changes and countless aspects, the human creations as the result of mental quest and aesthetics.

As the Director General of Antiquities and Cultural Heritage, I welcome with particular enthusiasm the exhibition policy of the Hellenic National Archaeological Museum which is the fruit of a modern concept, and I express my admiration and warmest wishes for the success of the Museum's project to present Beauty as perceived by the ancient Greeks, outside the place where it has resided for thousands of years, in beautiful places like China.

I would therefore like to thank and warmly congratulate in my capacity as a Director General of Antiquities and Cultural Heritage of the Hellenic Ministry of Culture all the institutions and people who supported the organizing of the exhibition and collaborated closely for its realization.

The new edition of the catalogue will be a valuable tool for visitors, researchers and art lovers alike, offering a deeper understanding of the meaning and evolution of the concept of Beauty as we expand its horizons in a global dialogue.

I hope that this publication will be an endless source of knowledge for the cultural and scientific community, but also a springboard for thoughtful discussions and studies.

In closing, I wish that the presentation of the exhibition will prove successful, that it will resonate with numerous visitors, that it will contribute the most to informing and raising public awareness, adding to our constant requests: protecting the past, but also securing the future of our cultural heritage.

致　辞

希腊国家考古博物馆董事会 主席

迪米特里奥斯·奥伊科诺穆教授

希腊国家考古博物馆与中国国家博物馆是世界上举足轻重的两大博物馆。我们经过长期深度合作，终于在北京联合推出了"美的多元——古希腊的艺术与生活"展。

继该展在雅典首展取得巨大成功后，双方自2020年起便着手筹备北京巡展计划。与此同时，该展的精简版本也在希腊多座城市巡展，不仅扩大了其影响力，更传达了展览的核心理念。

尽管由于新冠疫情危机和全球旅行限制一度令项目进展受阻，但两馆工作人员始终秉持初心，从未放弃。因此，作为希腊国家考古博物馆董事会主席，可以在此邀请中国国家博物馆的观众一同踏上这场美学探索之旅，我深感荣幸。

人类对美的追求是永恒而普遍的。在古希腊，自史前时期到奠定西方文明基石的各历史阶段，这种追求都得到了生动而具体的体现。无论是诗歌、文学、哲学，抑或是建筑、艺术乃至民主制度，皆为满足人们感官与心灵的双重需求而生。此次展览，我们从雅典精心挑选了279件展品，旨在引领观众通过美的表达，深刻感受古希腊文化世界的独特韵味。同时，我们诚邀观众跟随展览中的珍贵文物一同探寻那些激发个人或集体灵感的源泉，正是这些灵感铸就了永恒的美学杰作。

在此，我要向所有在希腊和中国为这一艰巨项目倾注心血、提供支持的工作人员致以最诚挚的谢意。我坚信，此次展览将对加强和深化希腊与中国之间的文化交流与合作发挥重要作用。

GREETINGS

Hellenic National Archaeological Museum, President of the Board

Prof. Dimitrios Oikonomou

Two of the most important museums of the world, the Hellenic National Archaeological Museum and the National Museum of China have worked together closely for a long period of time to present the exceptional archaeological exhibition "The Countless Aspects of Beauty in Ancient Art" in the Chinese capital.

The cooperation with a view to present the exhibition in Beijing started in 2020, immediately after the closure of its highly successful presentation in Athens. An abridged version of the exhibition also toured other Greek cities, further highlighting its impact and conveying its messages.

Due to the pandemic crisis and the worldwide travel restrictions the endeavor was suspended, but the idea never ceased to exist in the minds of the people of the two Museums. It is thus with great pleasure that, in my capacity as the President of the Board of the Hellenic National Archaeological Museum, I have the privilege and the honour to welcome the visitors of the National Museum of China to the aesthetic journey offered by the exhibition.

The search for Beauty, is a timeless human need and it was materialized during the Greek antiquity from Prehistory through the historical times in creations upon which the western civilization was established. Poetry, literature, philosophy, architecture, art, even democracy, have all been motivated by the need to create works offering satisfaction to both the senses and the mind. The 280 exquisite exhibits that have travelled the long journey from Athens to Beijing have been thoroughly selected to guide the visitors through the expression of Beauty to the perception of the ancient Greek world. At the same time, all these treasures presented in the exhibition invite the visitors to investigate into the roots of the personal or collective inspiration which resulted in these aesthetic achievements.

I would like to express my gratitude to all those who have worked and supported this demanding project both in Greece and China. I deeply believe that this exhibition will play a significant role to the enhancement and deepening of the cultural relations between the Hellenic Republic and the People's Republic of China.

前　言

中国国家博物馆 馆长
高　政

　　中国和希腊作为对人类文明演进作出奠基性重大贡献的文明古国，都有着极其丰厚的历史底蕴和令人无法抗拒的独特魅力，而这正源于中希两种相距遥远的文化所共有的包容性与创造性。与中华文明一样，古希腊文明在漫长的演进过程中，始终以一种开放包容的姿态，吸纳并融合周边文化的精华，从爱琴文明的萌芽，直至城邦时代的辉煌。"美"在这一过程中扮演着独特且无法替代的角色，它不仅催生了众多艺术杰作的诞生，也滋养了无数伟大哲学思想的发展。

　　"美的多元——古希腊的艺术与生活"展由中国国家博物馆和希腊文化部、希腊国家考古博物馆联袂推出，展示了希腊国家考古博物馆馆藏的279件（套）陶器、青铜器、金银器、玻璃器、壁画、雕塑等不同类型的珍贵文物。展览通过"寻美，永恒的主题""爱美，不变的天性""镌美，卓越的塑造""美，无尽的求索"四个单元，从古希腊充满艺术想象的日常用具、精美别致的妆容服饰，到令人叹为观止的人体雕塑，再现了新石器时代晚期至公元前1世纪近5000年的漫长历史中，古希腊对"美"这一主题的执着追求和多元创造；展现了"美"在古希腊精神世界中的独特地位，以及古希腊人通过对"美"的探索实现自我超越，并引导观众对"美"之于人类的特殊价值进行深入思考。

　　在当今世界，中希文明所蕴含的智慧对于人类破解时代难题、推动构建人类命运共同体有着独特的价值。希望本次展览，成为促进中希文明交流互鉴的重要典范，让文明之光在交相辉映中照亮历史、照鉴未来。

PREFACE

National Museum of China, Director

Gao Zheng

As civilizations that have made fundamentally great contributions to the evolution of human civilization, China and Greece both have extremely rich historical heritage. Their unique and irresistible charms stem from the inclusiveness and creativity shared by these two distant cultures. Like the Chinese civilization, the ancient Greek civilization has always been open and inclusive, absorbing and integrating the essence of the surrounding cultures, growing from the seeds of Aegean civilization to the glory of the Greek polis (city-states). "Beauty" plays a unique and irreplaceable role in this process, which not only gave birth to many artistic masterpieces but also nurtured the development of countless great philosophical ideas.

"The Countless Aspects of Beauty in Ancient Art" is jointly presented by the National Museum of China, the Greek Ministry of Culture, and the Hellenic National Archaeological Museum, including 279 pieces/sets of pottery, bronze, gold and silverware, glassware, murals, sculptures, etc. The exhibition features four sections, "Aesthetic Aeterna", "the Beautiful and Desirable", "Focusing on the Body", and "Endless Quest". The everyday objects that reveal the Greeks' artistic imagination, and the exquisite costumes and makeup to the stunning human sculptures illustrate the persistent pursuit and diverse expressions of "beauty" in ancient Greece during the nearly 5000-year journey from the Late Neolithic period to the first century B.C., highlighting the unique significance of "beauty" in the spiritual realm of ancient Greece and its role in self-transcendence, and inviting audiences to delve into the ultimate value of beauty.

In today's world, the wisdom contained in Chinese and Greek civilizations has unique value for mankind to tackle the problems of the times and promote the building of a community with a shared future for mankind. I hope that this exhibition will become an important example for promoting exchanges and mutual learning between Chinese and Greek civilizations, so that the light of the two shining ancient civilizations can shed light on the history and shine through the future.

前　言

希腊国家考古博物馆 馆长

安娜-瓦西莉基 · 卡拉帕纳约杜

2018年，我在担任阿卡迪亚文物管理局局长期间，有幸参观了希腊国家考古博物馆的"美的多元——古希腊的艺术与生活"展。该展由时任馆长、现任董事会副主席玛丽亚·拉戈吉亚尼·格奥尔加拉克斯博士精心策划。这是一次意义深远的展览，其重要性不仅体现在深邃的理念与直观的具象化表现上，更在于其所采用的现代博物馆学展示手法以及精心策划的多感官实验研讨上。2021年1月，我有幸接任希腊国家考古博物馆馆长一职，很高兴得知该展览此前已计划前往中国，在世界上非常重要的博物馆之一——中国国家博物馆展出。尽管新冠疫情带来了前所未有的挑战，筹备工作时间较原计划大幅延长，但本着精诚合作和高度专业的精神，我们最终克服了重重困难。今天，我很荣幸作为希腊国家考古博物馆馆长，与我的同事们，同时也是2018年展览的策展团队一起，在北京热忱欢迎各位的到来。

人类对美的追求，是创造力的重要源泉。本次展览精心布局，从多个维度对美学世界进行了深入剖析：第一部分聚焦日常物品中蕴含的创作者对美的独特理解；第二部分揭示美在人类外在形象演变过程中起到的强大作用；第三部分探讨与人体紧密相关的美的动态变化；第四部分则借助古希腊艺术之美，深入探索古希腊的精神世界。通过重新诠释古希腊艺术，希腊国家考古博物馆的精选藏品精准传达了展览的核心理念，并成功吸引了广大观众的目光。展览不仅实现了其教育功能，更在观众与古希腊艺术之间建立了牢不可破的纽带。在中国这一文化遗产极为丰富的国度，这一纽带的结成尤为重要。

有鉴于此，我要向所有在希腊和中国为此项目辛勤工作的同人表达诚挚的感谢。正是他们的不懈努力，才取得了今日的成就。同时，我还要衷心感谢希腊国家考古博物馆和中国国家博物馆的工作人员，感谢他们不懈努力，相互协作，共同克服重重困难。我坚信，本次展览将不仅成为两馆之间的里程碑，也将成为两国关系的里程碑。

PREFACE

Hellenic National Archaeological Museum, Director General

Dr. Anna Vasiliki Karapanagiotou

In 2018, as a Director of the Ephorate of Antiquities of Arcadia, I was one of the thousands of visitors of the temporary exhibition of the National Archaeological Museum "The Countless Aspects of Beauty in Ancient Art", which was curated by Dr. Maria Lagogianni-Georgakarakos, an esteemed colleague, then Director of the National Archaeological Museum and today, Vice President of its Board. It was a significant exhibition not only because of its profound concept and its materialization but also thanks to its modern museological approach and the multisensory experimental workshops which included. So, when I assumed the privileged position of the Director of the National Archaeological Museum in January 2021, I was excited to find out that the exhibition had already been scheduled to travel to China in order to be presented at the National Museum of China, one of the most important museums of the world. Though the preparations lasted much longer than we originally believed due to the unprecedented pandemic situation, we managed to overcome the difficulties in a spirit of excellent cooperation and high expertise. Thus, it is truly a great honour for me, today, as Director General of the Hellenic National Archaeological Museum, that I welcome you at the exhibition here, in Beijing, together with my colleagues, the same team of people who had prepared the exhibition in 2018.

Based on the principal idea that human creativity is the result of the irresistible need to captivate Beauty, the exhibition unfolds several aspects of the aesthetic world by following an articulated rationale. The first section presents the approach of everyday life objects which reflect the concept of Beauty of their creators. The next section is devoted to the powerful effect of the importance of Beauty in the evolvement of the image of the human appearance. The third section focuses on the dynamics of Beauty in relation to the human body while the fourth section offers the chance to gain insight the spirit of the ancient Greek world through the Beauty of the ancient Greek art. Thus, the excellent objects selected among the treasures of the Hellenic National Archaeological Museum to convey the concept of the exhibition succeed in engaging the audience by presenting a revived interpretation of the ancient Greek art. Following this intellectual trail the exhibition achieves its educational role while at the same time evokes feelings and emotions which create an unbreakable bond between the visitors and the Greek antiquity. Such bond takes on even greater importance when it is cultivated in a country such as China with a huge cultural heritage.

Having all these in mind I would like to express my gratitude to all those who worked hard both in Greece and China so that we are able to present such an excellent result. Warm thanks are also due to the staff of both the Hellenic National Archaeological Museum and the National Museum of China for their continuous effort to collaborate and resolve problems and difficulties. I am sure that this exhibition will constitute a landmark for the relations not only between the two museums but also between the two countries.

希腊国家考古博物馆简介

希腊国家考古博物馆作为希腊历史最悠久且规模最大的考古博物馆，珍藏着全球范围内重要的古希腊艺术品。

博物馆的历史与现代希腊的国家历史密不可分。它的主要使命是保护与展示19世纪从希腊各地征集而来的珍贵文物。随着希腊文物发掘工作的不断深入和私人收藏家的慷慨捐赠，博物馆逐渐成为希腊最重要的考古博物馆。时至今日，其馆藏数量已超过11 000件（套），全面展现了自公元前7000年史前时期至公元5世纪古典晚期古希腊文化的独特魅力与风貌。

博物馆矗立于一座宏伟的新古典主义建筑之中，由当时德国知名建筑师路德维希·朗格设计，后又经恩斯特·齐勒完善。这座建筑始建于1866年，是雅典市内保存完好且极具19世纪特色的建筑之一。历经20世纪的扩建与翻新，如今展厅面积达8000平方米，每层楼均设有数十个展厅以供参观。

希腊国家考古博物馆包括以下五个常设展馆。

一、史前文明馆：涵盖公元前7000年至约公元前1050年，希腊大陆及各岛屿主要文明的代表性文物，如迈锡尼皇家陵墓中的黄金珍宝、著名的基克拉迪小雕像以及保存完好的锡拉壁画等。

二、雕塑馆：作为全球同类收藏中规模最大且最重要的一处，展出了来自希腊各地以及希腊世界的1000件艺术品，时间跨度自公元前7世纪至公元5世纪，重点展品包括青年库罗斯雕像、少女科莱雕像，以及殡葬和建筑纪念雕塑等。

三、花瓶和小型艺术品馆：展示了公元前11世纪至罗马时代古希腊陶器艺术的代表作，陶土小雕像，珍贵的金、银和玻璃收藏，公元前5000年至拜占庭时期晚期的斯塔萨托斯收藏，以及包含史前时代到希腊化时期的776件作品的弗拉斯托斯-塞尔皮埃里斯收藏。

四、青铜器馆：包含大量独一无二的原作，如海神波塞冬神像和来自"安提凯希拉沉船"的"安提凯希拉"机械装置，该装置为保存至今最早的便携式天文计算器，可追溯至公元前1世纪。

五、埃及馆：因其重要性而享誉全球，其展品全面再现了埃及文明的全貌，年代跨度自公元前5000年的前王朝时期至罗马帝国时期（公元前30—395年）。

在其悠久的历史中，希腊国家考古博物馆在文物保护领域做出了巨大贡献。其目前设有三个工作室和一个化学实验室，采用最新方法对各种材料的文物进行保护。

博物馆一直致力于推动考古研究的发展，成为世界各地考古学家的研究中心，还积极参与国际项目并制作特别的教育节目。此外，博物馆还拥有丰富的图片档案、以考古出版物为重点的图书馆、演讲厅以及临时展览区。

希腊国家考古博物馆旨在向国际推广古希腊文明的历史、文化和艺术价值，积极组织并参与在希腊及世界各主要博物馆举办的临时展览。

HELLENIC NATIONAL ARCHAEOLOGICAL MUSEUM

The Hellenic National Archaeological Museum is the oldest and the largest archaeological museum in Greece and houses the most important collections of ancient Greek art in the world.

The history of the National Archaeological Museum is inseparable from the history of the Modern Greek State. Its primary mission was to protect and exhibit antiquities that were being collected throughout Greece in the 19th century. It gradually became the most prominent archaeological museum of Greece and was enriched with excavation finds from all areas of the Greek world, as well as with antiquities donated from private collectors. Today its rich collections, enumerating more than 11000 exhibits, offer the visitor a unique panorama of the ancient Greek culture from the dawn of Prehistory in the 7th millennium B.C. to the Late Antiquity (5th century A.D.).

The museum is housed in an imposing Neoclassical building, initially designed by Ludwig Lange and later formed by Ernst Ziller, both renowned German architects of their time. The building was founded in 1866, and is one of the most characteristic 19th century buildings still preserved and admired in Athens. It was extended and renovated throughout the 20th century and today the exhibition areas include dozens of galleries on each floor and cover an area of 8000 square meter.

The Hellenic National Archaeological Museum houses five major collections of antiquities, permanently exhibited in its grounds:

The Collection of Prehistoric Antiquities comprises representative artefacts of the major civilizations that flourished in the Greek mainland and the islands from the 7th millennium B.C. to ca. 1050 B.C., including the gold treasures from the royal tombs at Mycenae, the famous Cycladic figurines and the excellently preserved wall paintings from Thera.

The Sculpture Collection is the largest and most important of its kind worldwide, exhibiting 1000 unique works of art from all areas of Greece and the Greek world, dating from the 7th century B.C. to the 4th century A.D. Highlights include statues of male Kouroi and female Korai, and an array of funerary and architectural monumental sculptures.

The Vases and Minor Art Collection displays representative works of ancient Greek ceramics from the 11th century B.C. up to the Roman era, terracotta figurines, valuable collections of gold, silver and glass masterpieces, as well as the Stathatos Collection that covers a timespan from 5th millennium B.C. to the Late Byzantine period and Vlastos-Serpieris Collection that comprises 776 works, spanned from the Prehistoric to the Hellenistic period.

The Metalwork Collection comprises a large number of unique original artefacts, most notably bronze figurines and statues like the Artemision Poseidon, and displays the world-famous "Antikythera Mechanism" from the Antikythera Shipwreck, one of the earliest preserved portable astronomical calculators dating to the 1st century B.C.

The Collection of Egyptian Antiquities, internationally renowned for its significance, includes antiquities representing the full spectrum of the Egyptian civilization, dating from the early Predynastic period (5000 B.C.) to the time of the Roman Empire (30 B.C.–395A.D.).

Throughout its long history the Hellenic National Archaeological Museum has contributed immensely to the evolution of the archaeological conservation science and today it houses three conservation laboratories and a chemical laboratory employing the latest methods in conserving antiquities of all materials.

The Museum is dedicated to promoting archaeological research, functions as a research center for scientists across the world, participates in international projects and produces special educational programs. It includes a rich photographic archive, a library focused on archaeological publications, a lecture theater and an area assigned to temporary exhibitions.

The Museum aims to enhance internationally the historical, cultural and artistic values of the ancient Greek civilization and, to serve this purpose, it organizes and participates in temporary exhibitions in major museums in Greece and countries all over the world.

The Hellenic National Archaeological Museum is going through a new historical phase, as the planned building expansion and overall upgrading of the existing historic building are a great challenge to achieve its new exhibition goals and reformed functions at all levels.

目　　录
CONTENTS

爱美，不变的天性
The Beautiful and the Desirable

镌美，卓越的塑造
Focusing on the Body

尾声：美，无尽的求索
Epilogue: Endless Quest

图　版

CATALOGUE OF WORKS

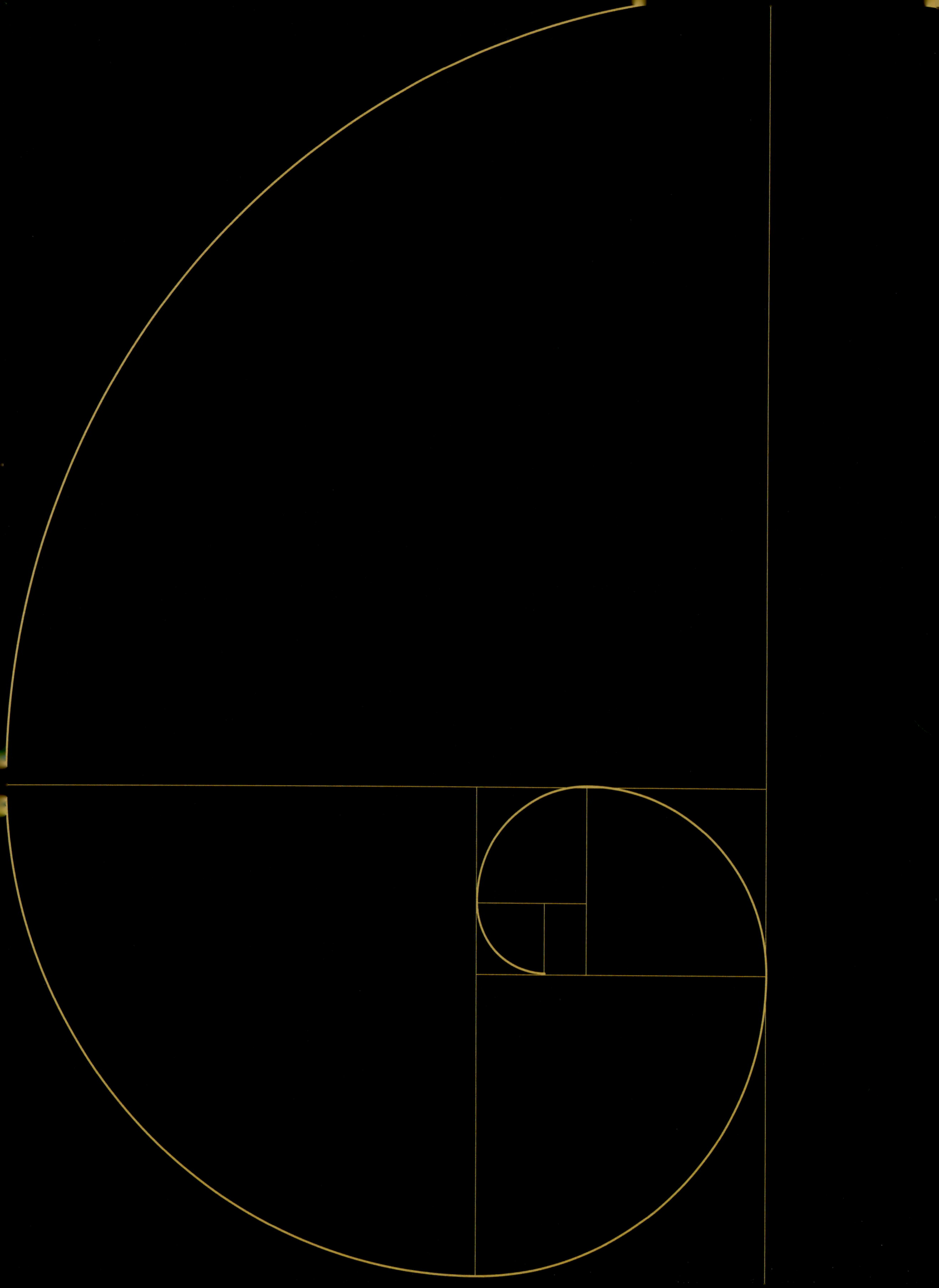

序

章

A FEW WORDS
ABOUT THE EXHIBITION

美是一个神秘而迷人的概念，数千年来，对人类的心灵有着无限吸引力，并与之相伴随形。美，在感官上令人愉悦而难以抗拒。它体现在每个时期的艺术中，也以其不断的变化和多元的表达在人类创造中刻下自己的印记。本次展览聚焦于古希腊造物的美学维度，同时也邀请观众一同探寻审美选择背后的精神底色。

展览将沿着"美"——这条贯穿人类创造力历史进程的线索，通过四个部分展开：

"寻美，永恒的主题"，本单元将展示古希腊不同历史时期的日用器皿，这些器具为我们呈现了人类历史发展中审美的持续变化及其不同侧面。

"爱美，不变的天性"，本单元试图借助古希腊神话中对美的诠释，以及考古发掘中与古希腊服装、发型和妆饰相关的物证，对古希腊社会的审美偏好进行本质上的探讨。

"镌美，卓越的塑造"，本单元展示了从新石器时代到希腊化时期，对人体视觉表达的演变，以及其中所蕴含的美。

展览的尾声部分"美，无尽的求索"，旨在引导观众对美的内涵及其对人类的特殊价值进行深入的哲学思考。

Enigmatic and charming, beauty as a concept captivates the human mind and accompanies it through the centuries. Appealing and pleasing to the senses, beauty is perceptible in the art of all periods, sealing with its constant alternations and its countless aspects of the human creation. The exhibition focuses on and highlights the aesthetic dimension of the ancient works, inviting at the same time the spectator to look for the spiritual basis of aesthetic choices.

The exhibition narrative unfolds in four parts, unraveling the thread that transcends human creativity: Beauty.

In "Aesthetica Aeterna" we see on display selected objects of everyday life that record the continuous alternations and different facets of aesthetics in human diachrony.

"The beautiful and the desirable" attempts an essential approach to the aesthetic preferences of the ancient societies on the basis of what the ancient Greek myths reveal about beauty and the archaeological finds that relate to clothing, hairstyles and beautification.

The third part titled "Focusing on the Body" illustrates the expression of beauty in the visual rendering of the human body from the Neolithic period to Historic times.

At the end, "The endless quest" aims at the aesthetic contemplation on the significance of the beautiful and its value for humans.

OOI

大理石女性头像浮雕圆盘残片

来自米洛斯岛 , 基克拉迪群岛

约公元前 460 — 前 450 年

Fragment of a circular marble relief with the head of a woman

From Melos, Cyclades

Around 460 – 450 B.C.

HNAM Γ 3990

　　圆盘上描绘的可能是爱与美的女神阿佛洛狄忒。她浓密的头发束成一个髻，卷曲地搭在修长的脖颈上。鬓角处可附上一绺金属卷发。这张脸庞散发着优雅与匀衡之美，

The goddess of beauty, Aphrodite, is perhaps depicted on the disc. Her rich hair is gathered in a sakkos (snood), which curves over the nape of the lean neck. An additional metal curl would be attached to the temple. The face emits grace and balanced beauty,

不同音调

产生最美的和谐

——赫拉克利特

（约公元前535——前475）

from differences results

the most beautiful harmony

Heraclitus (c.535-475 B.C.)

寻美，永恒的主题

1

SECTION I .

AESTHETICA AETERNA

　　材质与造型的无数种变化更迭，构成了丰富的艺术视觉词汇。古希腊文明中，于不同时代、不同文化环境中诞生的美学形态组成了一幅迷人的画卷，这其中不仅蕴含了数之不尽的"美"的不同版本，而且展现出人类为了在对立中创造和谐之美而做出的努力。即便是在最平凡的日常器具中，我们也可以清晰地看到人类对艺术追求的不断变化。而这恰恰证明了，"美"是人类的普遍需求，人类永远不会停止以最富有想象力的方式去表达"美"。

Countless alternations in materials and forms compose the visual vocabulary of art. Prototypes of aesthetics from different periods and cultural environments reveal an enchanting picture that encompasses the innumerable versions of beauty, but also the effort of man to achieve harmony by binding opposites together. The perpetually changing landscape of artistic quests, even in objects of daily use, confirms that beauty is a universal human need, which will never cease to seek its expression in imaginative ways.

002

带有双色迪米尼风格装饰的陶碗

来自塞萨利地区的迪米尼

新石器时代晚期二期，公元前 4800—前 4500 年

Clay bowl with bichrome Dimini
style decoration

From Dimini, Thessaly

Late Neolithic II, 4800 – 4500 B.C.

HNAM II 5920

在这种由直线构成的网格状图案中，扭转的螺旋纹创造出了新的装饰美感，尤其适合在盛放液体时欣赏。

The torsion of the spirals integrated in a web of straight-line motifs creates new aesthetics in decoration, best appreciated when serving liquids.

003

陶罐

来自塞萨利地区的维斯维基马古拉

新石器时代晚期，公元前 5300 — 前 4500 年

Clay vessel

From Visviki Magoula, Thessaly

Late Neolithic, 5300 – 4500 B.C.

HNAM II 17353

　　这是一件手工制作的大型容器，装饰有花纹、圆圈和条带，突显了其造型。这件陶罐不仅美观，而且能通过它极高的价值增强拥有者的声望。

　　A large handmade vessel decorated with a combination of patterns, circles and bands accentuating its shape. This jar was not only aesthetically pleasing but also a prestige object of high value for its owners.

004

精工大理石罐，"坎迪拉"

来自基克拉迪群岛的帕罗斯岛

早期基克拉迪文化 一期，公元前 3200 — 前 2800 年

Marble elaborate vase, "kandila"

From Paros, Cyclades

Early Cycladic I, 3200 – 2800 B.C.

HNAM Π 4763

　　这些石罐以其硕大的尺寸、洁白的大理石光泽，及其在形态对称中体现的艺术价值，在基克拉迪社会中被视为尊贵之物。这类器皿主要用作富人墓葬中的随葬品。

Their impressive size, their white marble brightness and their artistic merit in morphological symmetry pinpoint the marble "kandiles" as prestige objects in Cycladic society. These vases were mainly used as funerary offerings in rich burials.

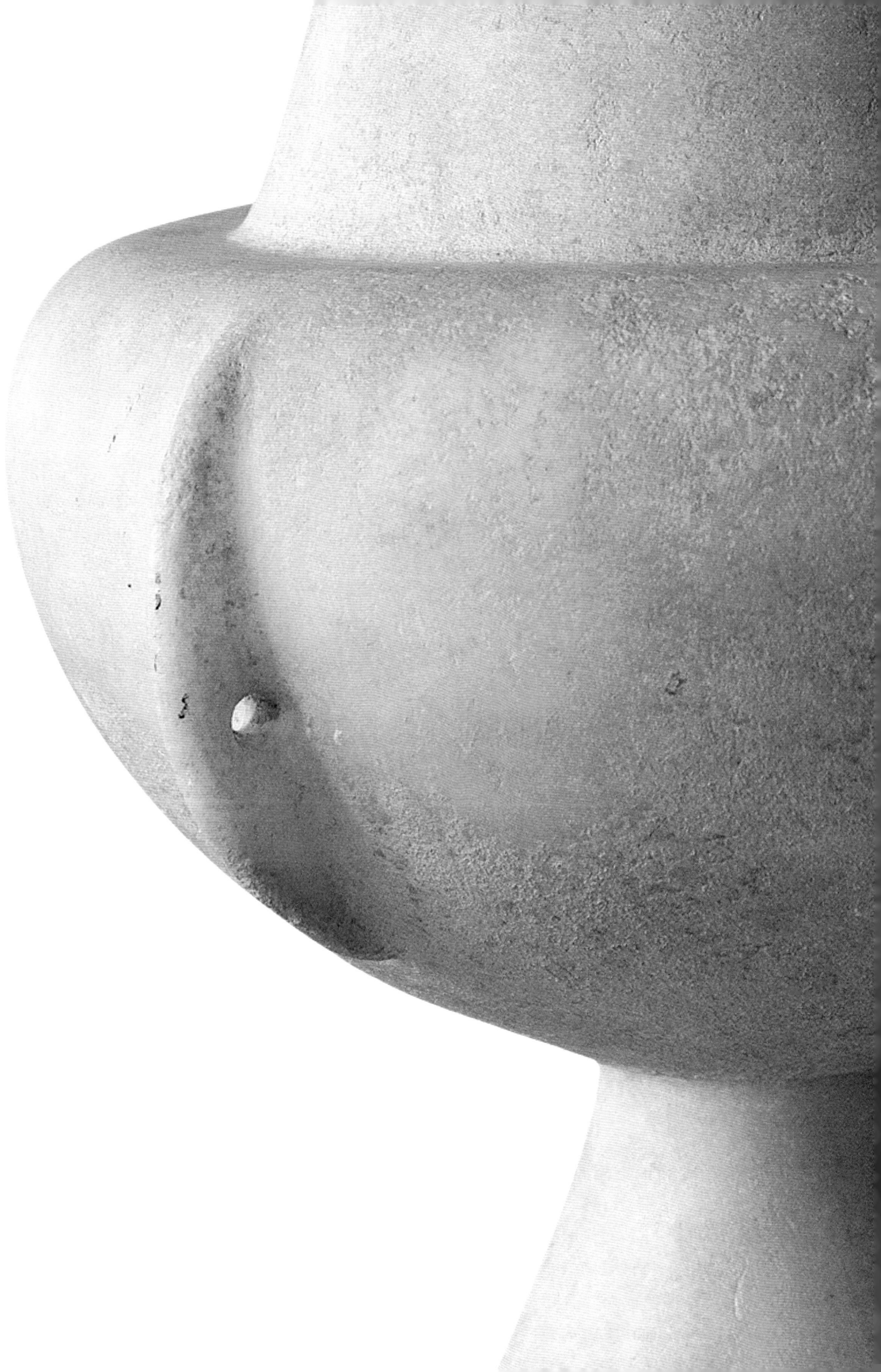

005

绿泥石平锅形器皿

来自基克拉迪群岛，可能是纳克索斯岛

早期基克拉迪文化二期，公元前 2800 — 前 2300 年

Frying pan vessel (made of chlorite schist)

Probably from Naxos, Cyclades

Early Cycladic II, 2800 – 2300 B.C.

HNAM Π 20935

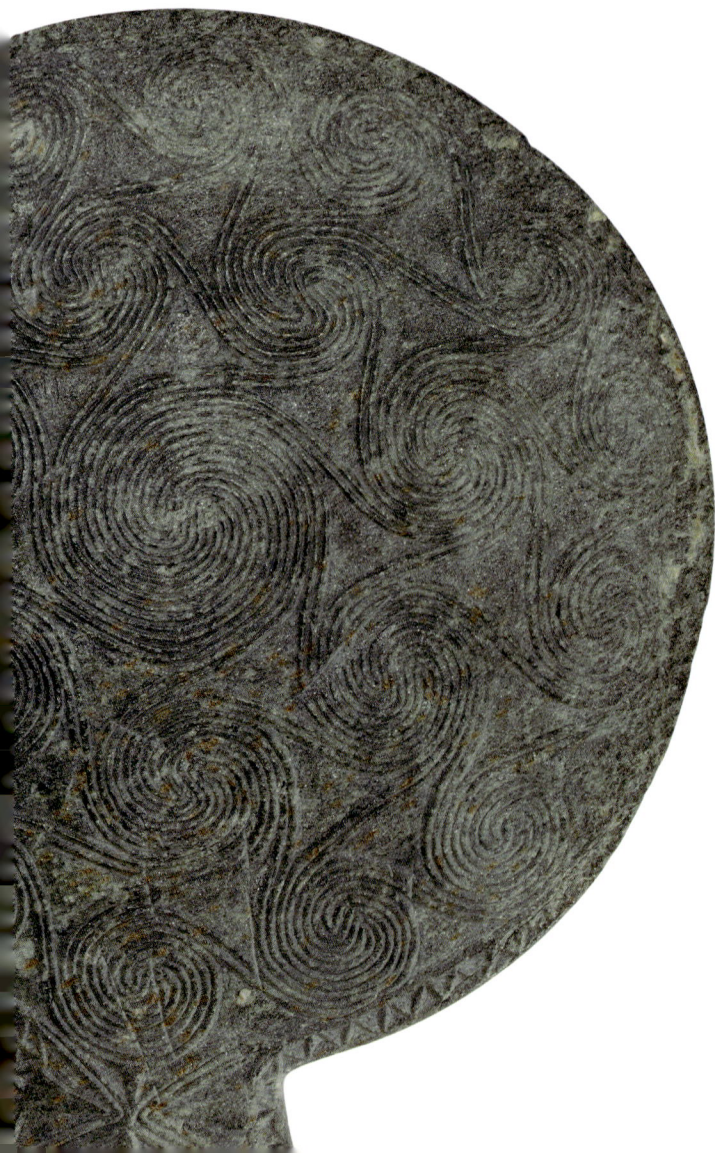

用大理石或其他石材制作的平锅形器皿十分罕见。这件文物通体布满涡形浅浮雕纹饰，这些精致复杂的装饰表现了基克拉迪群岛周围波涛汹涌、充满危险和挑战的海域。

Frying pan vessels made of marble or other stones are rare. The vessel is decorated with spirals in low relief. Its delicate decorations depict the rough seas, full of dangers and challenges, surrounding the Cycladic islands.

006

"船形陶器"

来自基克拉迪群岛，锡罗斯岛的查拉德里亚尼墓葬

早期基克拉迪文化二期，公元前 2800 — 前 2300 年

"Sauceboat"

From the Chaladriani cemetery, Syros, Cyclades

Early Cycladic II, 2800 – 2300 B.C.

HNAM II 5191

这是公元前三千纪典型的容器造型。这种容器被用来倾倒液体，在基克拉迪群岛及希腊大陆常有发现。优良的土质和高超的烧造技术使其拥有极薄的器壁。

A typical vase shape of the 3rd millennium B.C. Evidently a pouring vessel, commonly found in the Cyclades, as well as in mainland Greece. Its clay and firing are of excellent quality forming particularly thin walls.

007

刻纹抛光红陶瓶（跨页左）
半球形刻纹抛光黑陶杯（跨页右）

来自塞浦路斯
公元前 2000 — 前 1800 年（陶瓶）
公元前 1900 — 前 1725 年（陶杯）

Incised red-burnished prochous and incised
black-burnished hemispherical cup

From Cyprus
2000 – 1800 B.C. (prochous)
1900 – 1725 B.C. (cup)
HNAM KYΠ 12046, HNAM KYΠ 12379

这是两件来自塞浦路斯的手作陶
器，经过抛光后光泽闪亮，表面有线状
刻纹，纹路中填充有白色石灰质材料。

Handmade vases, lustrous by burnishing,
decorated with incised linear motifs filled with a
white calcareous substance.

陶瓶长颈末端有小把手，以及带有穿孔的装饰块。陶瓶颈部
狭窄，瓶体呈葫芦状。

A small handle is found at the base of the neck and perforated decorative
lugs are distributed across the body. The vase with the very narrow neck and the
globular body imitates the shape of a gourd.

陶杯的外壁装饰有精巧的辐射状及圆圈状线条，白色的线条与黑色的表面形成了美妙的对比。

The outer surface of the cup is decorated with intricate linear radial and circular patterns, incised and filled with white lines making a beautiful contrast with its black lustrous surface.

008

圆锥形来通陶杯

来自基克拉迪群岛，米洛斯岛的费拉科皮

公元前 17 — 前 16 世纪

Clay conical rhyton-cup

From Phylakopi, Melos, Cyclades

17th – 16th centuries B.C.

HNAM Π 5735.1

受米诺斯陶器和多色装饰理念的影响，制陶师将花
萼形状的器型与所画的想象中的植物欣欣向荣的生长状
态完美结合，构成了一件富有想象力的作品。

Inspired by the Minoan ceramic repertoire and the decorative
concept of polychromy, the potter matched the calyx form of the
vase with the growth of plant motifs in an imaginary landscape.

009

陶壶

来自基克拉迪群岛，米洛斯岛的费拉科皮

公元前 16 世纪

Clay prochous

From Phylakopi, Melos，Cyclades

16th century B.C.

HNAM Π 5762

　　画师用两种颜色精心地绘制了鸟儿，辅以其他附加主题，用以装点这样一个日常使用的陶壶。

The vase-painter decorated a jug of everyday use with an admirable bichrome composition of birds and supplementary motifs.

010

陶壶

来自基克拉迪群岛，锡拉岛（今圣托里尼岛）的阿克罗蒂里

公元前 16 世纪

Clay prochous

From Akrotiri, Thera (Santorini), Cyclades

16th century B.C.

HNAM II 27570 [AKP 1838]

壶身上的水鸟体态十分优雅，画师用多种色彩绘制，并以飘带图案来划分画面的不同区域。

The painter depicts with grace the motion of the polychrome aquatic birds, which are placed in an extended decorative zone, defined by bands.

O11

喙口"乳钉"陶壶

来自基克拉迪群岛，锡拉岛（今圣托里尼岛）的阿克罗蒂里

公元前 16 世纪

Clay beak-spouted "mastoprochous"

From Akrotiri, Thera (Santorini), Cyclades

16th century B.C.

HNAM Π 27436 [AKP 877]

这是一种具有象征意义的容器，以简单抽象的方式结合了女性和鸟类的特征。壶嘴处绘有"眼睛"，壶颈装饰着两串项链，壶身上双乳高耸并被圆点围绕。这是在锡拉岛（今圣托里尼岛）火山爆发前制造的高质量陶器的绝佳范例。

A vessel of symbolic significance, combining female and bird features, in a simple abstract manner. The "eyes" are painted on the spout, a double necklace decorates the neck and the breasts are plastically rendered and painted on the body, encircled by dots. This is an extraordinary example of the high quality pottery manufactured on Thera at the time preceding the volcanic eruption.

012

带滤孔层的有盖陶罐

来自基克拉迪群岛，锡拉岛（今圣托里尼岛）的阿克罗蒂里

公元前 16 世纪

Strainer pyxis

From Akrotiri, Thera (Santorini), Cyclades

16th century B.C.

HNAM II 27574 [AKP 2650]

这件华丽的容器内部有滤孔层，用于制作芳香油或在宗教仪式中作为香炉使用。罐身装饰有涡形图案和白色圆点，底座的番红花图案则让人联想到锡拉岛（今圣托里尼岛）的美景。

Luxurious vessel with incorporated strainer. It was used for the production of perfumed oils or as an incense-burner in rituals. Spirals and white dots decorate the body of the vase, while the crocus flowers evoke the beauty of the Theran landscape.

013

百合和番红花纹杯

来自基克拉迪群岛，锡拉岛（今圣托里尼岛）的阿克罗蒂里

公元前 16 世纪

Cup decorated with lily and crocus flowers

From Akrotiri, Thera (Santorini), Cyclades

16th century B.C.

HNAM Π 27420 [AKP 505]

　　花蕊和花朵的轮廓用红色着重勾勒。装饰集中在杯子外壁的一侧，方便左手持杯的使用者在饮用时欣赏，从而带来视觉和其他感官的多重享受。

　　The stamens and outlines of the flowers have been highlighted in red. The decoration is confined to the side that was visible to a left-handed drinker, in order to indulge the sight as well as the other senses.

014

麦穗纹锥形带嘴杯

来自基克拉迪群岛，锡拉岛（今圣托里尼岛）的阿克罗蒂里

公元前 16 世纪

Spouted conical cup decorated with ears of barley

From Akrotiri, Thera (Santorini), Cyclades

16th century B.C.

HNAM II 27496 [AKP 1290]

　　大麦是珍贵的谷物，成熟的麦穗仿佛在这件容器壁上轻轻摇曳。将描绘自然界充满动感、栩栩如生的彩绘与器物的立体造型巧妙地结合起来，是锡拉岛（今圣托里尼岛）陶器的一大特征。

　　The ripe ears of this precious cereal seem to rustle gently on the surface of the vessel. The lifelike, full-of-motion rendering of the natural world is in harmony with the three-dimensional object: a characteristic of Theran pottery.

015

鸟巢形滑石碗

来自基克拉迪群岛，锡拉岛（今圣托里尼岛）的阿克罗蒂里

公元前 16 世纪

Steatite bird's nest bowl

From Akrotiri, Thera (Santorini), Cyclades

16th century B.C.

HNAM II 27569 [AKP 1835]

　　花瓣形的浮雕如同有生命般，蔓延并环抱着碗身，体现出传统米诺斯风格石制器皿的特征，这在当时的爱琴海地区非常受欢迎。

　　Relief petals are shown growing and embracing the body of the vase, in the characteristic fashion of the long Minoan tradition of these stone vessels, which were very much loved in the Aegean of their time.

016

金杯

来自伯罗奔尼撒半岛，迈锡尼的"墓圈 A"，4 号竖井墓

公元前 16 世纪

Gold cup

From Mycenae, Grave Circle A, shaft grave IV, Mycenae, Peloponnese

16th century B.C.

HNAM Π 442

捶打而成的花瓣状装饰围拢着杯壁，突出了金杯花萼形的器型，为使用者带来意趣。这件有凹槽的华丽金杯曾与另外19件金银器皿一同被献给一位年轻的"王子"，从而构成了希腊历史上已知最古老的宴饮酒具套装。

The hammered petals of the decoration give prominence to the calyx-shaped body of the vase, thereby arousing the interest of its user. The luxurious fluted vase had been offered to a young "prince" together with 19 gold and silver vases, thus comprising the oldest known set of symposium vessels in the Greek world.

017

金浅杯

来自伯罗奔尼撒半岛，登德拉的第 10 号室墓

公元前 16 — 前 15 世纪

Gold shallow cup

From chamber tomb 10, Dendra, Peloponnese

16th – 15th centuries B.C.

HNAM Π 8743

这是一款装饰有常春藤叶图案和浮雕饰带的典雅酒杯。有证据表明它曾在王宫中被作为日常生活器具使用，而后又成为奢华的王族墓葬的一部分。

An elegant drinking cup decorated with an embossed frieze of ivy leaves. It was evidently used in life and later deposited as a grave offering in a lavishly furnished royal burial.

018

滑石灯

来自伯罗奔尼撒半岛，迈锡尼的室墓

公元前 14 世纪

Steatite lamp

From a chamber tomb at Mycenae, Peloponnese

14th century B.C.

HNAM II 3125α

米诺斯人在照明器具方面的制造传统随着石制花萼形灯的发明而达到顶峰。这种造型的灯通常在边缘装饰有螺旋和其他图案，一旦被点燃，便如同发光的花朵。

The Minoan tradition in vessels of lighting peaked with the invention of stone calyx-shaped lamps: often decorated on the rim with spirals and other motifs, once lighted, they would look like glowing flowers.

019

圆陶盒

来自伯罗奔尼撒半岛，迈锡尼遗址第 7 号室墓

公元前 14 世纪

Clay pyxis

From chamber tomb 7 at Mycenae, Peloponnese

14th century B.C.

HNAM Π 2257

这件精美的器皿来自米诺斯文化的克里特岛，盒盖上装饰着一朵大玫瑰花，盒身围绕着一圈飞鸟和花卉图案。这种器皿常用来珍藏珍贵的珠宝、化妆品或药品。

Imported from Minoan Crete, this exquisite vessel was decorated with a large rosette on the lid and a frieze of flying birds and floral motifs on the vessel body. Such vessels contained precious jewellery, cosmetic or medicinal substances.

O20

"繁复海洋风格"的马镫柄陶罐

来自阿提卡地区，佩拉蒂公墓

公元前 12 世纪

Clay stirrup jar of the "Closed Marine Style"

From the cemetery of Perati, Attica

12th century B.C.

HNAM Π 9151

这件贵重的器皿最终被用于陪葬，罐子里曾装有某种珍贵的液体。罐身密集地装饰着多种多样的几何图案，最引人注目的是罐身两侧各绘有一只巨大的章鱼，鸟和鱼仿佛围绕着章鱼游动。

A valuable vessel ultimately used as a funerary gift, this stirrup jar contained some kind of precious liquid. It was densely decorated with a variety of geometric motifs and most conspicuously a large octopus on each side with birds and fish seemingly swimming around it.

O21

装饰有几何图案的陶酒壶

来自阿提卡地区的帕拉亚科基尼亚

约公元前 750 年

Geometric oenochoe

From Palaia Kokkinia, Attica

Ca. 750 B.C.

HNAM A 18472

壶身上装饰着各种几何图案，像刺绣一样覆盖了整个表面。乳状突起使酒壶象征女性躯体，而壶身的花纹正如她身着的华服。

The vase is richly adorned with geometric ornaments, which cover, like embroidery, the entire surface. On the shoulder two mastoid projections convert the vase into an aniconic indication of a woman-like body lavishly dressed.

022

陶迪诺斯罐

来自塞浦路斯

公元前 750 — 前 600 年

Clay dinos

From Cyprus

750 – 600 B.C.

HNAM A 12356A

尽管像这样的敞口容器通常被用于烹饪或调酒，但它们优雅的造型、精致的彩色装饰无不表明，高级的审美情趣不仅体现在华丽的仪式器皿上，而且已经融入了人们的日常生活。

Although open vessel shapes like dinos or lebes, were used for cooking or mixing wine, their elegant shape and their elaborate, colourful decoration indicate that high aesthetics were not limited to luxurious ritual vessels, but became an integral part of everyday life as well.

023

盖子上有四匹马的圆盒

来自雅典的克拉米科斯公墓

公元前 750 — 前 735 年

Pyxis with four horses on the lid

From Athens, Kerameikos cemetery

750 – 735 B.C.

HNAM A 17972

这个布满几何图案的大圆盒的主人可能来自上层社会，圆盒提手位置的四匹骏马象征着地位和财富。

The large-sized pyxis, full of geometric patterns, possibly implies the upper social class its owner belonged to, since the horses in place of a handle indicate status and affluence.

024

带盖青铜水罐

来自塞萨利地区特里卡拉的帕拉约加迪基

公元前 540 — 前 530 年

Bronze pitcher (hydria) with lid

Palaiogardiki, Trikala, Thessaly

540 – 530 B.C.

HNAM X 18232

　　这件器皿由科林斯的作坊精心制作而成。其垂直手柄被制成裸体青年的样子，手柄与罐身的连接处则点缀着狮身人面兽、棕榈叶和公羊。"Hydriae"（水罐）有陶制的也有金属制的。它们主要用于家庭生活中运送液体，但也用于祭祀仪式、净化仪式和其他仪式中。它们还用作骨灰瓮，更罕见地用作颁发给为纪念英雄或神灵而举行的比赛获胜者的奖品。

Made with special care by a corinthian workshop. The vertical handle is in the shape of a nude youth (kouros), ending to a palmette, rams and sphinxes. Pitchers (hydriae) were made in both clay and metal. They were mainly used for transporting liquids in domestic life, but also in sacrifices, purification rites and other rituals. They also served as cinerary urns and more rarely as prizes awarded to the winners of contests held in honour of a hero or deity.

025

白色细颈有柄油瓶

来自优卑亚岛（今埃维亚岛）的埃雷特里亚

由萨布罗夫画师创作

公元前 455 — 前 440 年

White lekythos

From Eretria, Euboea island

By the Sabouroff Painter

455 – 440 B.C.

HNAM A 12747

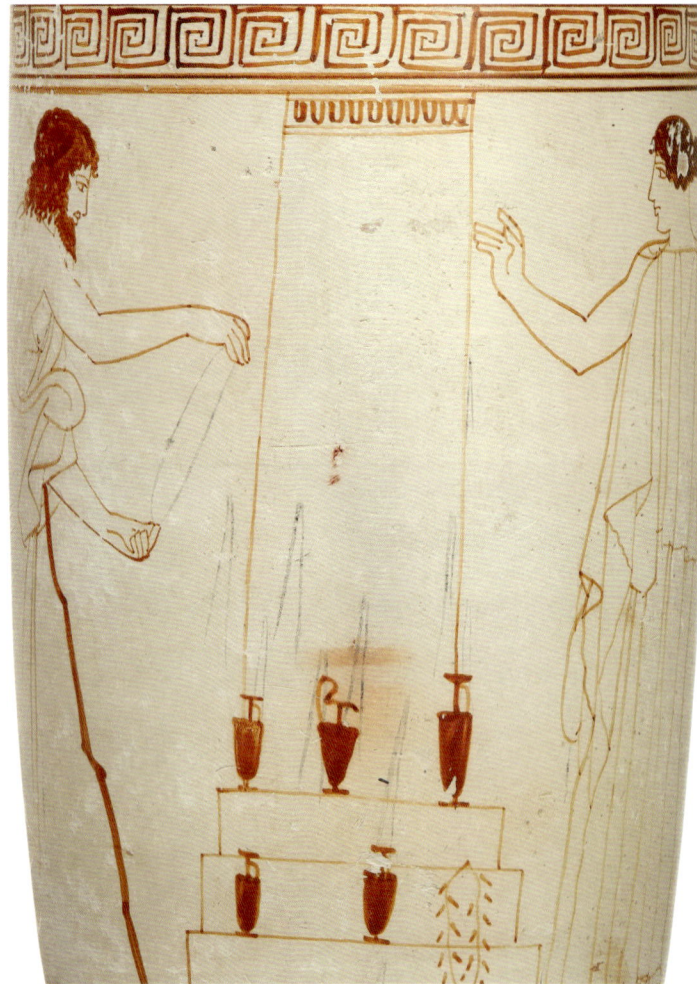

瓶身上，一男一女正在拜谒一座坟墓。男子挂着拐杖，手持绶带或花环，用以装点墓碑。另一侧，女子举手示意，目光投向正在全神贯注祭拜的男子。墓碑前还摆放着其他祭品。

A man and a woman are visiting a tomb. The man, who is leaning on a walking-stick, is holding a ribbon or a thick wreath, in order to decorate the stele. On the other side, the woman is raising her hand in a gesture, while she is looking towards the man who seems committed to his duty. In front of the stele other offerings are presented.

026

黑底红画陶迪诺斯罐

来自雅典的圣道区域

由迪诺斯画师创作

公元前 420 — 前 410 年

Red-figure dinos

From Athens, Area of Iera Odos

By the Dinos Painter

420 – 410 B.C.

HNAM A 14500

酒神狄俄尼索斯，在追随他的山和森林之灵萨提尔以及酒神狂女迈那得斯的陪同下，狂欢起舞。他的象征——酒神权杖在罐身的构图中占主导地位，宣告着神的全能，让所有不屈服于他的人陷入神圣的癫狂状态。罐身上的动物们则象征着这位葡萄酒之神（葡萄种植神）与大自然之间的原始联系。

The god Dionysus is accompanied by his troop of satyrs and Maenads, in ecstatic dance. Its symbol, the thyrsos, predominates in the representation, declaring the omnipotence of the god, who drives into sacred frenzy whoever does not surrender to him. Animals denote the primordial connection of the god of the vine with Nature.

027

阿提卡黑底红画陶水罐

来自优卑亚岛（今埃维亚岛）

公元前 375 — 前 350 年

Attic red-figure hydria

From Euboea island

375 – 350 B.C.

HNAM A 1424

爱神厄洛斯正站在酒神狄俄尼索斯和两位酒神狂女之间，用他的水瓶浇灌鲜花（可能是罂粟花）。花朵之美呼应了双翼爱神的美丽，而浇灌花朵的动作则象征着旺盛的生育能力。

Eros, among the god Dionysus and two Maenads, is watering flowers (possibly poppies) with his hydria. The beauty of the flowers is associated with the beauty of the winged god, while watering implies fertility.

028

银桶

来自塞萨利地区维莱斯蒂诺镇皮拉夫特佩丘的马其顿墓葬

公元前 3 世纪

Silver bucket

From the Macedonian tomb of Pilaf Tepe, at Velestino, Thessaly

3rd century B.C.

HNAM A 12079

银桶缺失的手柄与桶身的连接处，装饰着披着狮子皮的赫拉克勒斯浮雕头像。

One of the attachments of the missing handles is decorated with a relief head of Herakles wearing a lion's pelt.

029

银制芳香油瓶

来自塞萨利地区卡尔季察的"帕拉约卡斯特罗秘藏"

公元前 1 世纪

Silver alabastron

From the so – called "Palaiokastro Hoard", Karditsa, Thessaly

1st century B.C.

HNAM Xρ. 946

瓶身周围装饰的镀金浮雕体现了人们对酒神狄俄尼索斯的崇拜，酒神信徒们的形象环绕着瓶身。

An impressive gilded relief decoration of Dionysiac thiasos (followers of Dionysus) runs around the surface of the vessel.

030

带盖的黑底红画双耳喷口混酒器

来自希腊中部的维奥蒂亚

公元前 420 — 前 410 年

Red-figure calyx-krater with lid

From Boeotia, Central Greece

420 – 410 B.C.

HNAM A 1383

器身上，夜晚，黎明女神厄俄斯驾驶着她的战车，在赫尔墨斯的引领下越过海洋，象征黑夜转换成白昼，黑暗让位给光明。

On the body of the vase, Eos, the goddess of dawn drives through the night with her chariot over the sea. Eos, preceded by Hermes who shows her the way, alludes to the transition of night to day, as darkness surrenders its place to light.

031

淡蓝绿色棱纹玻璃碗

来源未知

公元前 1 世纪

Ribbed bowl of light bluish green glass

Unknown provenance

1st century B.C.

HNAM A 12522

这种类型的器皿在当时被用作仪式礼器或饮酒
器具。

This type of vessel was used for conducting ritual acts or as drinking vessel.

秉承阿佛洛狄忒的古老秘诀

In keeping with

the age-old secrets of Aphrodite

2

SECTION II .

THE BEAUTIFUL AND THE DESIRABLE

从新石器时代到古代晚期的文物，展示了人类对美经久不衰的渴望。遵循阿佛洛狄忒关于"爱美"（philokalia）的指令，以及神话中由她发明的美容秘诀，古希腊人开始使用美容工具、搭配服饰、佩戴珠宝、打造发型以及涂抹香膏等，以增加个人吸引力并彰显自己的审美偏好。自我装扮的工具往往小而精美，体现了不同时代的审美风潮。

Artefacts from the Neolithic period to Late Antiquity illustrate the diachronic desire of humans for the beautiful. In keeping with Aphrodite's commands about the love of the beautiful (philokalia) and the beauty secrets that, according to the Greek mythological episode related to the goddess Aphrodite , she first invented, the ancient societies made use of beautification kits, elaborate garments, masterfully fashioned jewels, spectacular hairstyles, perfumes and ointments, to enhance the desirable aspect of human nature and express their aesthetic preferences. The means that highlight beauty take often the form of small-scale masterpieces, revealing the elegant aesthetic prototypes of each period.

阿佛洛狄忒的诞生
THE BIRTH OF APHRODITE

根据赫西俄德的记载，天空之神乌拉诺斯的女儿、爱与美的女神阿佛洛狄忒是从海上的泡沫中诞生的。和她同行的是爱神厄洛斯和欲望之神希墨洛斯。女神一直来到塞浦路斯岛的海岸，才从海浪中现身。根据神话传说，在那里，时序女神荷赖和美惠三女神为她涂抹芳香油，穿上神祇的衣裙，佩戴上闪亮的饰品，之后将她带到奥林匹斯山。从那时起，她的使命就是为诸神和凡人提供爱欲。而根据荷马的记载，这位迷人的女神是宙斯和狄俄涅的女儿。

阿佛洛狄忒无与伦比的美将古代艺术带至了高峰，人们用生动而光彩夺目的方式记录她性感的形象。阿佛洛狄忒的形象有时与描述她历险的传说联系在一起，有时则与对她的崇拜联系在一起，她体现了女性美的精髓，象征着两性结合的生殖力量。在古希腊著名艺术家的作品中，不乏对阿佛洛狄忒的纪念性描绘，而其中最著名的是雕塑家普拉克西特列斯的作品，他是第一个刻画裸体阿佛洛狄忒的人。

Born from the foam of the sea, according to Hesiod, was Aphrodite, daughter of Uranus (the Sky). Her companions were Eros and Himerus (Desire). Having travelled as far as the shores of Cyprus, the goddess emerged from the sea waves. There, as mythological tradition has it, the Horai (the seasons of the year) and the Graces anointed her, dressed her in divine robes, adorned her with bright ornaments and led her to Olympus. Since then her allotted task was to offer erotic desire to gods and mortals. According to Homer, the bewitching goddess was the daughter of Zeus and Dione.

The unsurpassed beauty of Aphrodite transcends the ancient art that records in a vivid and glorious manner her sensual figure. Associated sometimes with legends narrating her adventures and at other times with her cult, the image of the goddess embodies the essence of female beauty and symbolizes the generative power of sexual union. Monumental representations of Aphrodite are encountered in works of famous artists of antiquity, with supreme among them the sculptor Praxiteles, who was the first to depict the nude body of the goddess.

032

沉睡的厄洛斯大理石小雕像

来源未知

公元 2 世纪

Marble statuette of a sleeping Eros

Unknown provenance

2nd century A.D.

HNAM Γ 5753

爱神厄洛斯被刻画成一个小男孩，四肢圆润，睡在岩石上。厄洛斯中分的辫子表示他尚且年幼。

Eros is depicted as a little boy, with chubby limbs, sleeping on a rocky surface. The braid along the central parting refers to his young age.

033

卡皮托利尼式阿佛洛狄忒雕像

来自原亚历山德罗斯·约拉斯收藏

罗马时代的作品，经历了古代和现代的多次修复

Statue of Aphrodite in the Capitolini type

From the former Alexandros Iolas Collection

A work of Roman times with numerous ancient and modern restorations

HNAM Γ 16151

这座雕像复刻于一件希腊化时代的作品（其原作被认为是普拉克西特列斯的《克尼多斯的阿佛洛狄忒》），由普拉克西特列斯的小儿子凯菲索托多斯于公元前300年左右所作。女神全身赤裸，发式繁复，双手羞涩地遮掩着胸部和下身。普拉克西特列斯的女性裸体范本因此而变得更为世俗和自然。这件雕塑在经过长期的清洁与保护工作，包括修复件内部组装方式的X光检测后，首次在希腊境外向公众展出。

The statue follows a Hellenistic version of the Cnidian Aphrodite of Praxiteles, assigned to his son, Cephisodotus the Younger and dated around 300 B.C. The goddess is depicted totally nude, with an elaborate headdress, covering prudishly with the hands her breasts and genitals. The Praxitelean model of female nudity has become more earthly and naturalistic. The statue is presented to the public outside Greece for the first time, after long cleaning and conservation works including the radiography of the internal assembly mode of the restorations.

最美女神的角逐
THE CONTEST FOR THE FAIREST ONE

最美丽的女神将获得奖品

The fairest of the goddesses shall get the prize

　　希腊神话中的"帕里斯的裁决"也许是自古以来的第一次选美比赛，胜者的奖品是一颗写着"献给最美丽的女神"的金苹果。这次比美是不和女神厄里斯精心设计的诡计，她因未能收到珀琉斯和忒提斯婚礼的邀请而怀恨在心，成功让赫拉、雅典娜和阿佛洛狄忒为金苹果争斗不休。特洛伊的帕里斯被宙斯任命为裁判，他最终选择了阿佛洛狄忒，只因为她承诺让帕里斯得到美丽的斯巴达王后海伦的爱。由此可见，美，一直都是最令人无法抗拒的礼物。

　　A golden apple bearing the inscription "to the fairest" was, according to the myth, the prize in the first ever beauty contest. It was a ploy used by the uninvited to Peleus and Thetis wedding, goddess Eris (Discord), to cause disarray among the guests, since, as a result, three goddesses, Hera, Athena and Aphrodite, competed for the title of the fairest one. Appointed as judge was Paris of Troy, who chose Aphrodite in exchange for the love of Beautiful Helen, queen of Sparta, confirming that beauty is the most desirable gift of all.

034

卢浮宫 / 那不勒斯式的阿佛洛狄忒大理石小雕像

来自伯罗奔尼撒半岛，埃庇道鲁斯的阿波罗 - 马利亚塔斯圣地

公元 1 世纪上半叶

Marble statuette of Aphrodite in the Louvre/Naples type

From the sanctuary of Apollo Maleatas in Epidaurus, Peloponnese

First half of the 1st century A.D.

HNAM Γ 1811

　　轻薄的长袍紧贴着阿佛洛狄忒的身体，布料的起伏巧妙地勾勒出了女性特征。她手中握着一个苹果，暗示她曾参与了帕里斯的裁决。此类雕塑的原型始创于公元前 420 年左右。

　　A thin chiton clings to the body selectively highlighting the anatomical signs of her femininity. The apple that she holds implies her involvement in the Judgement of Paris. The original of the type was created around 420 B.C.

035

阿提卡黑底红画陶护腿

来自优卑亚岛（今埃维亚岛）的埃雷特里亚

由克利俄画师创作

公元前 440 — 前 430 年

Attic red-figure epinetron

From Eretria, Euobea island

By the Clio Painter

440 – 430 B.C.

HNAM A 2383

这种护腿是典型的女性配饰。女性会在纺纱时将木制的护腿放在大腿上以辅助工作。这件装饰精美的陶制护腿可能是一件祈求神佑的供品，其上描绘了一处女性的区域。

The epinetron was a typical female accessory. Women placed plain wooden epinetra on top of their thigh, to facilitate them while they were spinning wool. This vessel decorated with scenes from the women's quarters, was probably a votive offering seeking for protection.

036

金头冠

来自塞萨利地区的"德米特里亚斯宝藏"

公元前 325 — 前 300 年

Golden Diadem

From the so - called "Demetrias Treasure", Thessaly

325 – 300 B.C.

HNAM Στ. 339

这件金头冠由形成藤蔓涡卷形状的螺旋金丝制成。中央部分装饰有赫拉克勒斯结和一个带翅膀的爱神厄洛斯。从结上垂下的是两条由三根金链构成的流苏，下方缀有石榴形状的坠饰。这件美丽的珠宝是一件随葬品，女主人曾头戴着它去往"彼岸"。

It is made of a spiral wire, shaping tendril scrolls. The Herakles knot decorates the central section with a winged Eros. Hanging from the knot are two tassels of three chains bearing schematic pomegranate pendants. This beautiful jewel adorned a woman's head and followed her to death.

妆容 BEAUTIFICATION

古希腊凡人女性对美的关注丝毫不逊于神祇，这种充满魅力与生命力的感官吸引力本就根植于女性的本质。而为了加强这种美的吸引力，古希腊女性会使用化妆品来完善自己的外貌。有时"交际花"们为了引人注目，会在脸上涂抹过量的化妆品，甚至因此常常成为喜剧诗人戏谑的对象。从古典时期到拜占庭时期的史料中可见，尽管社会对女性使用化妆品持强烈反对态度，但化妆品仍然是女性日常生活中不可或缺的"伴侣"。

Concern for beautification was as great for ancient Greek mortal women as it was for the gods, since the divine part of allure and the power to give life is inherent in feminine nature. The use of make-up by women to enhance their appearance and the reaction this elicited among men is evidenced through the sources. Hetaerae to impose their presence, used excessive quantities of make-up on their faces, and for this were the subject of teasing commentary from comic poets. Despite the strong disapproval of women using cosmetics found in the sources from the Classical period until Byzantine times with the acrimonious commentary by the Church Fathers, cosmetics were nevertheless women's inseparable companion.

037

黑底红画细颈有柄油瓶

来自阿提卡地区的维拉尼德扎

公元前 470 — 前 460 年

Red-figure lekythos

From Velanideza, Attica

470 – 460 B.C.

HNAM A 1624

瓶身绘有一位端坐着的衣着华贵的年轻女子，她对着镜子，正在熟练地整理发带，为自己打造更加迷人的外表。

A seated young woman, wearing impressive clothes, is looking at a mirror, while she arranges her headband with her hand in a familiar gesture, to improve her image, as she prepares herself for an enchanting appearance.

038

青铜镜

科林斯作坊作品，来源未知

公元前 450 — 前 425 年

Bronze mirror

From corinthian workshop, unknown provenance

450 – 425 B.C.

HNAM X 7575

镜柄的造型为一位穿着厚重外袍（佩普洛斯）的女人，她伫立在一个圆形底座上。镜面的边缘环绕着鸟类和玫瑰形装饰。

The mirror disc has a handle in the form of a woman wearing a heavy tunic (peplos) and resting on a circular base. The periphery of the disk is adorned with birds and a rosette.

039

阿尔戈斯作坊的青铜镜

来源未知

公元前 460 — 前 450 年

Bronze mirror from argive workshop

Unknown provenance

460 – 450 B.C.

HNAM X 7579

此青铜镜的镜柄为一个女性形象，下方连接在一个圆形底座上。镜面边缘环绕着玫瑰和动物形装饰。镜柄上，两个带翅膀的爱神环绕着下方中央的女子。

The handle of the mirror is in the form of a woman resting on a circular base. Rosettes and animals adorn the mirror disk periphery. The female figure is surrounded by two winged Eros.

040

尼克塞诺斯画师风格的阿提卡
黑底红画陶罐

来自埃伊那岛

约公元前 500 年

Attic red-figure pelike, in the
manner of the Painter of Nikoxenos

From Aegina island

Ca. 500 B.C.

HNAM A 1425

陶罐一侧描绘了一位裸体女子，她左手拿着梳子，正在一个有喷泉的门廊下沐浴。陶罐另一侧则描绘了一名潜伏中的重装步兵。

On one side, a nude woman, holding a comb in her left hand, is bathing in a fountain porch. On the other side a hoplite is lurking.

041

黑底红画双柄浅杯

来自希腊中部的维奥蒂亚

公元前 500 — 前 490 年

Red-figure kylix

From Boeotia, Central Greece

500 – 490 B.C.

HNAM A 1409

　　杯内底部描绘了一个年轻的裸体戴冠男子，他正用一个放在他大腿上的大盆洗手，盆的另一边则搭在一堵看不见的墙上。这些用于个人清洁的便携器皿常常与年轻人在竞技场的生活联系在一起。

In the interior of the vase a young nude crowned man is depicted, washing his hands in a large basin that rests on his thigh, while its edge is leaning against an imaginary wall. Individual portable vases that were used for cleanliness were linked to the life of young people in the Gymnasium.

042

金质微型带盖双耳罐

来自伯罗奔尼撒半岛，迈锡尼"墓圈A"3号竖井墓

公元前 16 世纪

Gold amphoriskos with lid

Grave Circle A, shaft grave III, Mycenae, Peloponnese

16th century B.C.

HNAM II 84

这件小巧器皿的瓶身由上下两部分黄金薄片拼接而成。底部有三个刻线同心圆装饰，提手周围则装饰着浮雕花朵。

其精细的制造和精美的装饰体现了工匠在金银细工方面娴熟的工艺、经验和知识，据推测由米诺斯文明时期的工匠所制，可能用于存放一些贵重的化妆品。

The body of the amphoriskos (small amphora) is composed of two sections constructed of thin gold sheet. Three incised concentric circles decorate its base while repoussé flowers adorn the space between handles.

Its manufacturing and elaborate decoration testifies to a craftsman with expertise, experience and knowledge in goldsmithing, probably a Minoan. It was likely used in storing some precious cosmetic substance.

043

微型化妆盒形金吊坠

来自伯罗奔尼撒半岛的登德拉

公元前 14 世纪

这只精美的微型化妆盒曾属于一位迈锡尼贵族女性。在盒中发现了疑似化妆品或药品的物质残留，经推测为某种香水或面部化妆品。若用链子穿过悬挂孔，既可以使其变成吊坠，又能同时封住盖子，以防其中所盛的珍贵之物意外洒出。

Gold pendant in the form of a small pyxis

From Dendra, Peloponnese

14th century B.C.

HNAM II 7350

In this tiny luxury pyxis (cosmetic box) that belonged to a Mycenaean noblewoman, residues of a cosmetic or medicinal substance, possibly perfume or face paint, were found. Through the suspension holes passed the chain that turned it into a pendant and at the same time sealed the cap so that the precious contents would not spill by accident.

044

金“耳勺”

来自伯罗奔尼撒半岛的登德拉

公元前 15 — 前 14 世纪

在迈锡尼贵族的化妆品套装中，“耳勺”是最为奢侈精致的工具。这件金“耳勺”很可能被用于少量挖取、混合或涂抹化妆品。

Gold "ear-pick"

From Dendra, Peloponnese

15th – 14th centuries B.C.

HNAM II 2883

Within the toiletry set of the Mycenaean elite, the luxurious "ear-pick" stands out as the most delicate tool. It was most probably used for the extraction of a minimal quantity, the mixture and perhaps the application of cosmetic substances.

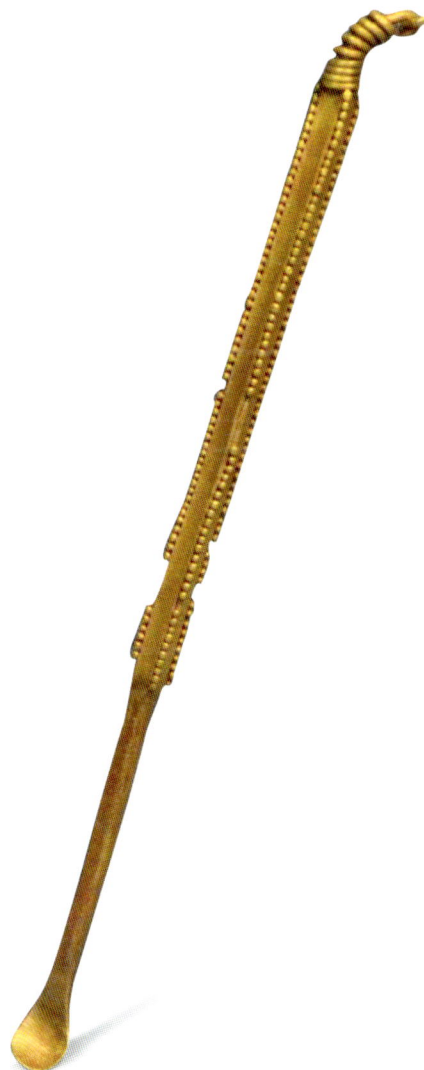

045

黑底红画带盖化妆盒

来自雅典

公元前 410 — 前 400 年

Red-figure pyxides with lids

Athens

410 – 400 B.C.

HNAM A 13676α, HNAM A 13676β

图中，较大的化妆盒上描绘了女性生活的区域，较小的化妆盒上则描绘了一些动物图案，盒盖上绘有三名女子的头像。这些化妆盒内装有用于美白肌肤的铅白粉。

On the larger pyxis a depiction of women's quarters is preserved, while on the small one animals are represented on the body, and three female heads on the lid. The vases contained psimythion, a lead-based powder that whitened the skin, making the face flawless.

046

大理石化妆盒

来源未知

公元前 430 年

Marble pyxis

Unknown provenance

430 B.C.

HNAM A 2381

这只带有底座的化妆盒属于古典时代最精致的一类大理石容器。这类容器主要用来盛放珠宝或化妆品，其精致的造型可能受到了木制原型的启发。

This marble pyxis with pedestaled foot belongs to the most elaborate category of classical marble vessels. These vessels served primarily as containers for jewellery or cosmetics and their elaborate shapes were probably inspired by wooden prototypes.

047

青铜折叠镜

来自优卑亚岛（今埃维亚岛）的埃雷特里亚

公元前 380 — 前 370 年

Bronze folding mirror

From Eretria, Euboea island

380 – 370 B.C.

HNAM X 7417 + 7418

　　镜子有两个盖子，每个盖子上都饰有浮雕，分别描绘了骑在马上和天鹅上的阿佛洛狄忒。古希腊的镜子上经常装饰着与阿佛洛狄忒相关的主题。

　　The mirror has two covers, each one adorned with a relief depiction of Aphrodite, seated on a horse and a swan respectively. Themes relevant to Aphrodite often decorate ancient mirrors.

048

半裸的阿佛洛狄忒小陶像

来自优卑亚岛（今埃维亚岛）的埃雷特里亚

公元前 3 世纪

Terracotta figurine of semi-nude Aphrodite

From Eretria, Euboea island

3rd century B.C.

HNAM A 4137

　　阿佛洛狄忒坐在岩石上，手持折叠镜。披肩（希玛纯）覆盖了她的下半身。这尊陶像呈现了爱与美的女神在审视镀金镜子中自己的样貌后，目光移开的一瞬间。

Terracotta figurine of Aphrodite seated on a rock, holding a folding mirror. Her himation covers her lower body and legs. The goddess of beauty is represented at the moment she has withdrawn her gaze from her image on the gold-plated mirror.

049

青铜折叠镜

来源未知

约公元前 260 年

Bronze folding mirror

Unknown provenance

Ca. 260 B.C.

HNAM X 16366

表面抛光的镜盖上是一位发型精致、佩戴珠宝的女性头像，呼应着使用铜镜的女性的美貌。

A female bust with elaborate hairstyle and jewels adorns the cover of the polished surface which mirrors the female beauty.

050

红底黑画细颈有柄油瓶

来自希腊中部的维奥蒂亚

公元前 500 — 前 490 年

Black-figure lekythos

From Boeotia, Central Greece

500 – 490 B.C.

HNAM A 12271

瓶口上引人注目的铭文"伊皮农"（HIPINON）说明了它的用途，即用于保存一种在古代广泛流传、香味持久且易于制备的香料。这种香料也被用来入药。

The vase preserves a remarkable inscription engraved on the lip, HIPINON, stating its destination. It was meant for keeping in it a fragrance of widespread circulation in antiquity, long lasting and easy to prepare. A fragrance of pharmaceutical use, too.

051

玻璃和条纹大理石芳香油瓶

分别来自雅典、埃雷特里亚以及未知地点

公元前 4 世纪

Alabastrons of glass and alabaster

From Athens, Eretria and of unknown provenance respectively

4th century B.C.

HNAM A 15005, HNAM A 12189, HNAM A 17343

这些装有没药（芳香油）的容器最早出现在古风时代。除了陶土外，人们也会用更贵重的材料制作这样的容器，以便保存对环境条件非常敏感的芳香油。将其中的内容物涂抹在男性身体上，可使其免受晒伤以及其他外伤。

These vessels, containing myrrh (perfume), first appeared in archaic times. Apart from clay, such vases were also made of more valuable materials, suitable for the preservation of sensitive perfumes. Their content was used to protect the male body from the sun as well as from injuries.

052

阿提卡黑底红画芳香油瓶

来自阿提卡地区

公元前 470 — 前 460 年

Attic red-figure alabastron

From Attica

470 – 460 B.C.

HNAM BΣ 24

瓶身描绘了住宅中女性区域的景象。两位女子穿着传统长裙（希顿），披着披肩（希玛纯），且头戴发饰。左边的女子举起镜子，右边的女子拿着芳香油瓶。两人之间放着一个装满羊毛的篮子，画面右侧有一棵棕榈树。

A depiction of Gynaeceum (women's quarters). A pair of women dressed in chiton, himation, and a headdress. The one on the left raises a mirror while the other on the right holds an alabastron. Between them a wool-basket full of wool, and on the far right edge of the scene is a palm tree.

053

阿提卡黑底红画芳香油瓶

来自雅典

公元前 470 — 前 460 年

Attic red-figure alabastron

From Athens

470 – 460 B.C.

HNAM BΣ 27

　　瓶身装饰分为四部分，描绘了女性世界。上方的女子分别身着长裙（希顿），披着披肩（希玛纯），其中一位手持镜子。下方的其中一位女子手持火炬，另一位是胜利女神，她正朝右走去。

　　The decoration of the vase is divided in four parts, with depictions of the feminine world. Above, women enveloped in chiton and himation, one of them holding a mirror. Below, a woman holding torches and Nike moving to the right.

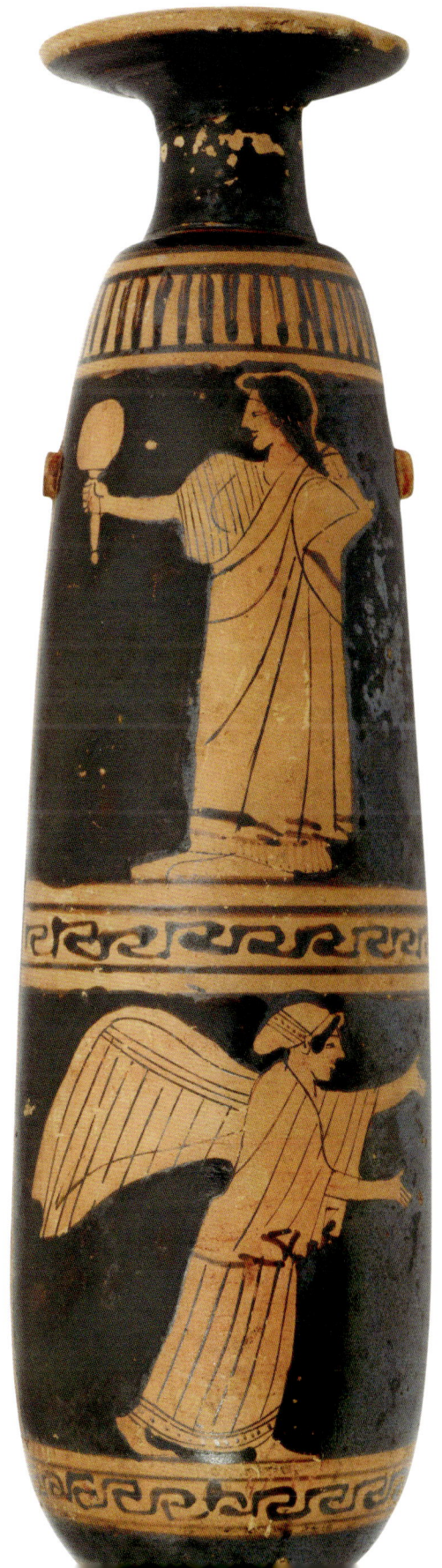

054

带细棍的金色圆柱形盒子

来源未知

罗马时期

Golden cylindrical case with a spathe

Unknown provenance

Roman period

HNAM Xρ. 96

055

黑底红画细颈有柄长油瓶

来自雅典

公元前 470 — 前 460 年

Alabastrons red-figure lekythos

From Athens

470 – 460 B.C.

HNAM A 1199

瓶子的用途在瓶身图案中显而易见。端坐的雅典女子一只手拿着芳香油瓶，另一只手拿着一根细棍将没药（芳香油）涂抹在身上。

The use of this object becomes apparent in the iconography of the vase. The seated Athenian lady holds in one hand an alabastron and in the other a stick, the spathe, which was used for applying the myrrh (perfume) to the body.

服饰 CLOTHING

　　自人类文明起源之时，服饰就不只是御寒蔽体的身外之物，也是每个人内在个性和品位的精神外化。每个人对服饰的选择都是一种自我彰显，而在古希腊，这种选择也更多地受到性别、年龄、社会地位、职业以及所处文化的影响。

　　古希腊服饰多为长袍样，通过文献与文物可以推断，在荷马时代，人们就已经开始穿着名为"佩普洛斯"的典型"多立亚"式服装。其后又出现了爱奥尼亚加顿和希玛纯等不同风格、不同穿着方式的服装。

Since the dawn of human civilization, clothing has not only served as a means to keep warm and cover the body, but has also been an external manifestation of one's inner personality and taste. Everyone's choice of attire is a form of self-expression, and in ancient Greece, this choice was more profoundly dictated by factors such as gender, age, social status, occupation, and the culture in which one lived.

In ancient Greece, clothing was predominantly in the form of robes. Based on written sources and depictions on artifacts, it can be inferred that during the Homeric era, people had already begun to wear the typical "Doric" type of clothing, known as the peplos. Subsequently, different types and styles of wearing clothes emerged, such as the Ionic chiton and the himation.

056

金质图章戒指

来自伯罗奔尼撒半岛，登德拉的第 10 号室墓
公元前 14 世纪

Gold signet ring

From chamber tomb 10 at Dendra, Peloponnese
14th century B.C.

HNAM Π 8746

戒面呈现了一个宗教场景：衣着华丽的女祭司或信徒正在走向顶部饰有献祭之角的神殿。戒圈非常窄小，即使是纤细的女性手指也难以戴上，因此这件珠宝可能是作为吊坠来悬挂佩戴的。

The bezel of the ring is decorated with a cult scene involving priestesses or worshipers in rich attire approaching a shrine topped with horns of consecration. The ring is very narrow, even for a slim female finger, so the jewel may have been worn suspended, as a pendant.

057

捧盒女子形金吊坠

来自伯罗奔尼撒半岛，迈锡尼的"墓圈 A"
公元前 14 世纪

Gold pendant in the shape of a woman holding a box

From Grave Circle A, Mycenae, Peloponnese
14th century B.C.

HNAM Π 2946

尽管这件饰品很小，但艺术家仍精心刻画出了女子的头饰和她背后的长辫子。

Despite the miniature scale of the ornament, the artist attributed the lady's diadem and her long braid down the back.

058

带有水晶头的青铜别衣针

来自伯罗奔尼撒半岛，迈锡尼的"墓圈 A"
公元前 16 世纪

Bronze pin with a rock-crystal head

From Grave Circle A, Mycenae, Peloponnese
16th century B.C.

HNAM Π 102

这种类型的别衣针由早期迈锡尼精英所使用，可能在特殊场合佩戴。

Dress pins of this type were used by the first generations of Mycenaean elite and were probably worn on special occasions.

059

带着婴幼儿的女子陶像（儿童养育者）

来自伯罗奔尼撒半岛，迈锡尼的室墓

公元前 14 世纪

Female figurine with baby and infant (kourotrophos)

From a chamber tomb at Mycenae, Peloponnese

14th century B.C.

HNAM Π 2493

此陶像身着长袖外衣，头戴头巾，辫发，体现了典型的迈锡尼女性服饰。女子怀里的婴儿被某种遮阳物或伞状物保护着。

The long-sleeved tunic, the head cover and the braided hair of the figurine form the typical Mycenaean female attire. The infant on the woman's back is protected by a kind of shade or umbrella.

060

浮雕装饰金盘

来自伯罗奔尼撒半岛，迈锡尼的"墓圈 A"

公元前 16 世纪

Gold discs with embossed decoration

From Grave Circle A, Mycenae, Peloponnese

16th century B.C.

HNAM Π 4, HNAM Π 8, HNAM Π 9, HNAM Π 13,

HNAM Π 14, HNAM Π 20

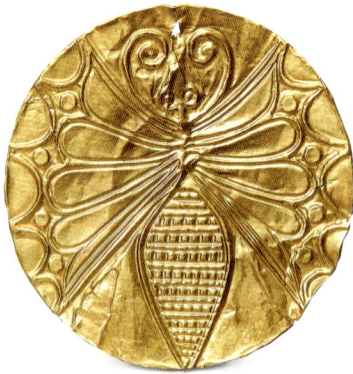

正如这些雕刻着与生命循环相关纹饰的随葬珍宝所体现的，早期迈锡尼统治者最喜欢使用的材料就是闪闪发光的黄金，不论生前或死后，这些黄金始终陪伴着他们。

The shining gold, a favorite material of the early Mycenaean rulers, accompanied them in life and in death, as indicated from the funerary jewellery with depictions associated with the cycle of life.

061

包金骨扣

来自迈锡尼的"墓圈 A"

公元前 16 世纪

Bone buttons covered with gold plate

From Grave Circle A, Mycenae

16th century B.C.

HNAM EAM Π 675, HNAM Π 679, HNAM Π 336

迈锡尼时代，男性和女性都会使用各种服饰配件，如金属腰带、扣环、别衣针、扣针，以及由各种材料制成的纽扣。

In Mycenaean times men and women used a variety of accessories for their garments, such as metal belts, buckles, pins and fibulae, as well as buttons made of various materials.

062

壁画残片

来自伯罗奔尼撒半岛，梯林斯卫城

公元前 13 世纪

Fragments of a wall painting

From Tiryns acropolis, Peloponnese

13th century B.C.

HNAM II 5878, HNAM II 5884

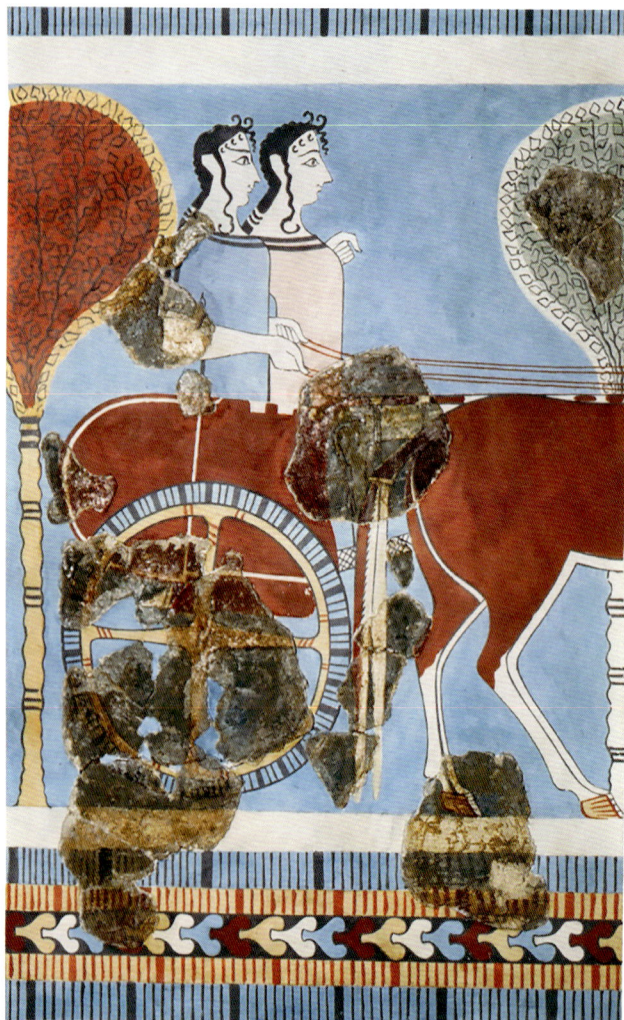

在右边的大壁画中，身着长袍的男女乘坐在战车上，他们皮肤白皙、发型精致，再现了考究的迈锡尼宫廷世界。而在左边的小壁画中，身着短袍的猎人正手持长矛前进。这些壁画残片来自一幅装饰在梯林斯王宫里的狩猎场景主题壁画，该场景中还包含战车、狗、野猪、鹿和自然景观等元素。

In the large fragment long-robed men or women, riding in a chariot, reproduce the standards of sophistication of the Mycenaean palatial world with the whiteness of their skin and hairstyles. In the smaller composition, hunters in short tunics advance holding spears. They come from a frieze that decorated the palace of Tiryns with a hunting scene that also included chariots, dogs, wild boars, deer and elements of the natural landscape.

063

鞋形陶制来通杯

来自阿提卡地区的格拉夫达

公元前 14 世纪

Clay rhyton in the shape of a shoe

From Glyphada, Attica

14th century B.C.

HNAM Π 8557

　　这对罕见而独特的鞋形陶制来通杯（一种用两个孔使液体分别进出的容器）模仿了西安纳托利亚风格满帮鞋的形状，鞋尖翘起。它最终被作为随葬品埋藏，证明其具有礼器用途。

　　This rare and individualistic rhyton (a vessel with two holes for in- and out- flowing) reproduces the shape of a closed shoe of Western Anatolian type with a raised tip. It was ultimately deposited as a funerary offering and had evidently ritual use.

064

陶瓶

来自希腊中部的维奥蒂亚

公元前 575 — 前 550 年

Clay vases

From Boeotia Central Greece

575 – 550 B.C.

HNAM A 2062, HNAM A 2063

这对芳香油瓶的形状是女性穿着凉鞋的脚。人们将珍贵的芳香油储存在这些形状各异的精美瓶子之中，为身体增添独特的气息。

Unguentaria in the shape of a female sandal-bearing foot. In these elaborate vases, appearing in various forms, delicate aromatic oils were stored, which provided the body with a distinctive identity.

065

右脚凉鞋陶模

来自克里特岛

公元前 575 — 前 550 年

Clay model of a right sandaled foot

From Crete island

575 – 550 B.C.

HNAM A 2072

这是一只穿着华丽皮凉鞋的女性脚部的模型，鞋带上装饰着棕榈叶。

Model of a female foot with a luxurious leather sandal, whose strap is decorated with a palmette.

066

维奥蒂亚扁平身体的小陶像

来自希腊中部，维奥蒂亚的塔纳格拉

公元前 575 — 前 550 年

Terracotta Boeotian flat-bodied figurine

From Tanagra, Boeotia, Central Greece

575 – 550 B.C.

HNAM A 4009

　　此陶像身着华丽的服饰，佩戴着石榴形吊坠项链，头戴高耸的头饰，是希腊早期表现女性妩媚风姿的塑像。

With ornate garments, necklaces bearing pomegranate pendants, and tall headdresses, the figurine is early expression of female coquetry.

067

阿提卡黑底红画双耳罐

来源不详

公元前 400 — 前 390 年

Attic red-figure amphora

Unknown provenance

400 – 390 B.C.

HNAM A 15113

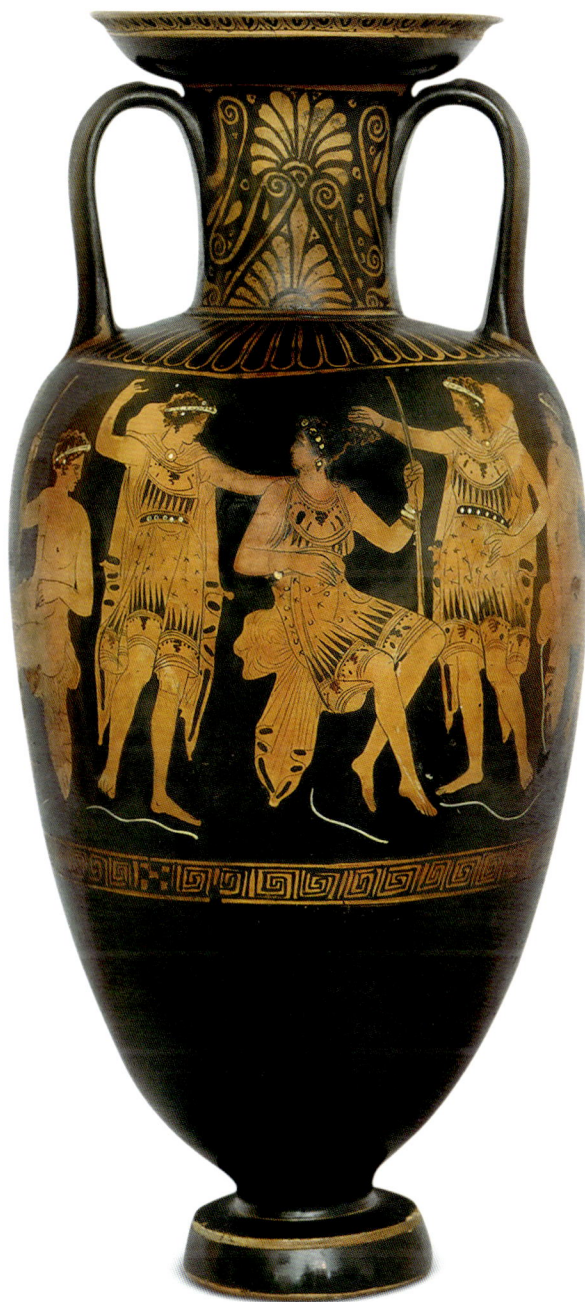

罐身主体描绘的是神话中的女英雄阿塔兰忒，她身着装饰华丽的短裙（短希顿），佩戴臂环和耳环，头冠点缀着她束起的发髻。她周围有四个年轻人，其中两个着旅人装束。

The mythical heroine Atalante wears a richly decorated short chiton, armlets, earrings, and a diadem which adorns her knotted hair. Around her four youths, two of them in travel attire.

068

女性小陶像

来自希腊中部，维奥蒂亚的塔纳格拉

公元前 260 — 前 190 年

Terracotta female figurine

From Tanagra, Boeotia, Central Greece

260 – 190 B.C.

HNAM A 4589

少女端庄地用长裙（希顿）和披肩（希玛纯）裹紧自己的身体，画笔细致地描绘了她的容貌，她一头红发，佩戴着圆形耳环，头戴一顶用于遮阳的托利亚式檐帽。

The maiden, modestly enveloped in her chiton and himation, has intensely painted features and red hair, while she wears round earrings and a tholia on her head to protect her face from the sun.

069

青铜别衣针

来自伯罗奔尼撒半岛，阿尔戈斯城的赫拉圣地

公元前 9 — 前 8 世纪

别衣针不仅是装饰品，还可以用于将衣服系在肩膀上，或用于悬挂项链。在圣所中，它们是献给神灵的供品，或用于固定神像的衣物。在墓葬中，它们则可能用于固定裹尸布。

Bronze pins

From the sanctuary of Hera at Argos, Peloponnese

9th – 8th centuries B.C.

HNAM X 20728/3, 11, 4, 13

Used for fastening garments on the shoulders or for suspending necklaces, along with their decorative character. In sanctuaries, they were gifts to the deities or fastened the garments of cult statues. In burials, they might have fastened the shroud.

070

银别衣针

来自雅典柏拉图学园的一座墓穴

公元前 1 世纪

爱神厄洛斯用情欲的陷阱俘获了凡人和神明。而在这枚别衣针上，他自己也成了俘虏，永远地坐在饰有浮雕叶饰和蜜蜂的柱顶上，半张着镀金的翅膀。

Silver pin

From a tomb in Plato's Academy, Athens

1st century B.C.

HNAM Xρ. 1083

Eros captures mortals and immortals in the traps of erotic desire. Here, a captive himself, he sits with his gilded wings half-open on a capital with relief foliage and a bee at the back.

071

四螺旋青铜胸针（扣针）

来源未知

公元前 9 — 前 8 世纪

这是一种特别的服装配饰，螺旋形状是原始的太阳象征。

Bronze brooch (fibula) with quadruple spiral

Unknown provenance

9th – 8th centuries B.C.

HNAM X 8197

An impressing garment jewel with spirals forming a primordial solar symbolism.

072

六枚弓形胸针（扣针）

来自阿提卡地区阿纳维索斯（金和银）和达迪 –
弗西奥蒂斯的古代的阿姆菲克利亚（青铜）

公元前 8 世纪 — 前 7 世纪初

Six bow brooches (fibulae)

From Anavyssos, Attica (gold and silver) and
ancient Amfiklia, Dadi Phthiotis (bronze)

8th – early 7th centuries B.C.

HNAM Χρ. 1515, HNAM Χρ. 1514, HNAM
X 16465, HNAM Χρ. 1516, HNAM Χρ. 1513,
HNAM Χρ. 1524

在这些胸针的扣板上，刻有几
何图案、"卍"字、鸟或蝎子。

The catch-plate engraved geometric
motifs, a swastika, a bird or a scorpion.

073

"8"形青铜胸针

来自希腊中部，马格尼西亚地区古菲赖的宙斯·陶
利俄斯和阿耳忒弥斯·埃诺迪亚圣地

公元前 8 世纪晚期

Bronze eight-shaped brooch

From the sanctuary of Zeus Thaulios and
Artemis Enodia at ancient Pherai, Magnesia,
Central Greece

Late 8th century B.C.

HNAM X 15872.1

胸针是一种实用的配饰，用于
固定服装或连接头饰和头巾的边缘。

Brooches were utilitarian pieces of
jewellery used as dress fasteners or to joining
the edges of diadems and head coverings.

074

黄金胸针（扣针）

来源未知

公元前 5 — 前 4 世纪

Gold brooches

Unknown provenance

5th – 4th centuries B.C.

HNAM Στ 259α, HNAM Στ 259β, HNAM Στ 259γ,

HNAM Στ 259δ

这是一种运用黄金造粒和锤揲工艺制作的首饰，其
拱形茎上饰有双锥形珠和小球体，末端饰有狮头浮雕
和飞马头状装饰。

Granular and hammered decoration with biconical beads and
globules on the arched stems. At its endings, an embossed head of
lion skin and a Pegasos bust.

075

阿提卡黑底红画双柄浅杯残片

来自雅典的克拉米科斯

约公元前 410 年

Fragment of an attic red-figure kylix

Kerameikos, Athens

Ca. 410 B.C.

HNAM A 20185

　　画面中，提莫克里特正准备把长裙（希顿）系在肩上。可以看到，她腿部的衣服上别着扣针。

A lady called Timokrite prepares to fasten her chiton on her shoulder. The brooch can be seen pinned to the garment on her legs.

076

无头女性雕像

来自基克拉迪群岛，提洛岛

公元前 520 — 前 515 年

Headless statue of a female figure

From Delos, Cyclades

520 – 515 B.C.

HNAM Γ 22

　　这尊颇具母性气质的雕像是一组神像中的一尊，被认为是女神勒托。她穿着华服、佩戴珠宝：精美的带袖长袍，垂褶的斜披斗篷，覆盖背部和肩膀的大披风、头巾，还有由圆形珠子和水滴状吊坠制成的项链。她的长发曾饰有金属螺旋发饰，在胸前呈波浪状发辫。

　　The mother-like figure is identified with Leto and belongs to a group of cult statues of gods. She wears rich garments and jewellery: a fine, long, sleeved tunic, a folded, obliquely draped cloak, a large overgarment (epiblema) covering her back and shoulders, a coif (kredemnon) on the head, a necklace made of spherical beads and drop-like pendants. The long hair forms wavy tresses on the breast, once decorated with metal hair spirals (sphekoteres).

077

大理石库罗斯（男青年）躯干

发现于雅典伊利斯索斯河的河床

公元前 5 世纪初

Marble torso of a kouros

Found in the bed of the Ilissos river, Athens

Early 5th century B.C.

HNAM Γ 3687

这尊男性雕塑披着一件覆盖背部的披肩（希玛纯），是为数不多的穿着衣服的库罗斯（男青年）形象之一。这种雕塑在希腊东部，尤其是爱奥尼亚地区很常见，这件作品也受到了该地区文化的影响。

The male figure, who wears a himation covering his back, is one of the few dressed kouroi. Most of them were common in east Greece, especially Ionia, by which the present piece is influenced.

078

带有浮雕装饰的女神德斯波伊娜（珀耳塞福涅别称）
大理石雕像所披披肩（希玛纯）局部

来自伯罗奔尼撒半岛，莱科索拉的"大女神"

德墨忒耳和德斯波伊娜（珀耳塞福涅）神庙

公元前 2 世纪初

Part of the marble himation of Despoina with relief
decoration

From the temple of the Great Goddesses, Demeter and Despoina, in

Lykosoura, Peloponnese

Early 2nd century B.C.

HNAM Γ 1737

这件雕塑模仿了考究的提花或刺绣织物，条状下摆
顺次装饰着神话人物和动物的形象。披肩上部的饰边主
要描绘了一组海洋神话人物。

The garment is imitating an elaborate patterned woven or
embroidered textile, adorned with miniature friezes of mythical
figures and animals in successive zones. The depiction of a marine
troupe predominates in the upper band.

首饰 与 发饰

JEWELLRY AND HAIR ORNAMENT

迄今为止发现的最早的人类珠宝是旧石器时代用贝壳制成的项链。新石器时代，真正意义上的加工首饰才出现，打磨过的石头、陶土、动物骨骼和贝壳是主要的原料。

米诺斯文明发展出了花丝和黄金造粒工艺，迈锡尼时期又出现了镂刻工艺。半宝石也让珠宝更添华光。古风时期和古典主义时期，凸纹、镂空、珐琅等工艺出现，希腊的珠宝制作工艺日臻精湛。

神灵，主要是女性神祇，都有精致的首饰和发型。发型与发饰的意义不仅在于区分性别，而在于表现个人与其所属社会之间的联系。对头发的护理和各种形式的美发手段，如剪发、剃发、染发或遮盖，都强调了个人在社会语境下身份和地位。

The earliest human jewellry discovered to date is a necklace made from shells dating back to the Paleolithic era. It was not until the Neolithic era that truly processed jewellry appeared, with polished stones, clay, animal bones, and shells serving as the primary materials.

The Minoan civilization developed the techniques of filigree and granulation in goldwork, and during the Mycenaean period, the technique of engraving emerged. Semi-precious stones also added luster to the jewellry. In the Archaic and Classical periods, techniques such as repoussé, chasing, and enamel began to appear, refining the art of Greek jewellry making to ever greater sophistication.

Deities, particularly female goddesses, are usually depicted with intricate hairstyles and accessories. Hair-dressing has a symbolic significance, not just for the differentiation between the sexes but mainly in respect to the bonds between individuals and the society to which they belong. Caring for the hair and all manner of hair intervention, such as cutting, shaving, dying, or covering, emphasize the participation, and at the same time subordination, of the individual in the social milieu.

079

人形石质吊坠

来自塞萨利地区

新石器时代晚期，公元前 5300 — 前 4500 年

Anthropomorphic stone pendant

From Thessaly

Late Neolithic, 5300 – 4500 B.C.

HNAM Π 6004.10

这是一枚由绿色片岩制成的简略女性形象的环形吊坠。

The female figure is depicted in schematic form as a ring-shaped pendant made from green schist.

080

黄金饰品

来源未知

新石器时代末期，公元前 4500 — 前 3300 年

Gold ornaments

Provenance unknown

Final Neolithic, 4500 – 3300 B.C.

HNAM Π 23324, HNAM Π 16683, HNAM Π 16690, HNAM Π 16689, HNAM Π 16691, HNAM Π 16686, HNAM Π 23325

不掺杂质的纯金光泽散发着永恒的美学吸引力。圆盘状、菱形以及条带状的黄金首饰会作为装饰品被缝在衣物上，与主人生死相随，黄金珠子则会被串成项链。工匠们将金片锤打成人们所需的形状，并在其上穿孔以便固定。

The unadulterated brightness of gold explains its timeless aesthetic attraction. Discs, lozenges and bands were sewn onto garments as ornamentation in life and death, while beads formed necklaces. Craftsmen hammered gold sheets, cut them into the intended shape and pierced attachment holes through them.

081

黄金珠宝吊坠

来源未知

新石器时代末期，公元前 4500 — 前 3300 年

Gold jewels-pendants

Provenance unknown

Final Neolithic, 4500 – 3300 B.C.

HNAM Π 16673, HNAM Π 16674, HNAM Π 16643,

HNAM Π 16641, HNAM Π 23311, HNAM Π 23312

　　新石器时期的珠宝虽然稀少，但地理分布广泛，而且都留有明显的使用痕迹。女性形象的环形小雕像或吊坠在希腊、巴尔干半岛和小亚细亚均有发现。菲勒斯（男性生殖器）形和鹿角状的吊坠较为少见，它们分别象征着男性的生育力以及每年春天自然界的万物复苏。

Neolithic jewels are rare, but they had a wide distribution and bear evidence of intensive use. Ring-shaped figurines or pendants schematically evoking the female figure were found in Greece, the Balkans and in Asia Minor. The phallus-shaped and animal antler pendants, less widespread, manifest the generative power of man and the rejuvenation of nature each spring.

082

贝壳环状饰品（异棘海菊蛤）

来自塞萨利地区的迪米尼

新石器时代晚期二期，公元前 4800 — 前 4500 年

Seashell rings (Spondylus gaederopus)

From Dimini, Thessaly

Late Neolithic II, 4800 – 4500 B.C.

HNAM Π 16625, HNAM Π 6007.4, HNAM Π 6007.6 (3 objects)

　　地中海异棘海菊蛤海贝可用于制作项链、手镯、脚链、发饰、腰带饰品甚至权杖头，是罕见的装饰品和尊荣的象征。这种贝壳主要采集于爱琴海，但贝壳及其制品远销至巴尔干半岛、中欧以及波罗的海地区。

Beads, bracelets, anklets, hair or waist belt ornaments, even scepter heads, were made from the Mediterranean sea shell spondylus gaederopus, as rare objects of ornamentation and prestige. Mainly collected in the Aegean, the seashells were transported as a raw material or finished product as far as the Balkans, Central Europe and the Baltic sea.

083

彩色宝石项链

来自基克拉迪群岛的帕洛斯岛

早期基克拉迪文化一期，公元前 3200 — 前 2800 年

Necklaces of coloured stones

From Paros, Cyclades

Early Cycladic I period, 3200 – 2800 B.C.

HNAM II 4882 (2 objects)

项链在基克拉迪文化中变得流行起来。这些彩色的宝石珠子是小型艺术品，往往带有与天体或繁衍周期相关的特殊象征意义。

Necklaces became popular in Cycladic society. These colorful stone beads are small works of art, quite often bearing special symbolism associated with the celestial bodies and the fertility cycle.

081

黄金圆片、青铜别针和镶嵌玻璃珠的青铜项链

来自塞萨利地区的塞斯克罗

希腊大陆青铜时代中期，公元前 1900 — 前 1600 年

Gold discs bronze pin and glass bead-mounted bronze necklace

From Sesklo, Thessaly

Middle Helladic period, 1900 – 1600 B.C.

HNAM Π 5912, HNAM Π 5913, HNAM Π 5914 (3 objects)

图中展现的是由青铜管状串珠和玻璃珠制成的项链以及两个黄金圆片（遮蔽纽扣或耳饰），是从该时期最富有的女性墓葬之一出土的饰品。

Necklaces of bronze tubular and glass beads and two gold discs, covering buttons or earrings, decorate one of the richest female burial of this period.

085

银手镯

来自爱奥尼亚海莱夫卡斯岛的斯特诺

早期希腊大陆青铜时代二期，公元前 2800 — 前

2300 年

Silver bracelet

From Steno, Leukas, Ionian Sea

Early Helladic II, 2800 – 2300 B.C.

HNAM II 6285

这只手镯由粗银线制成，两端为锥形，呈密集螺旋状。其可能被作为臂环来佩戴，后来成为女性墓葬中贵重的随葬品。

Bracelet made of thick silver wire with conical edges and dense spiraling. Probably worn as an armlet, it became the precious burial offering to a female.

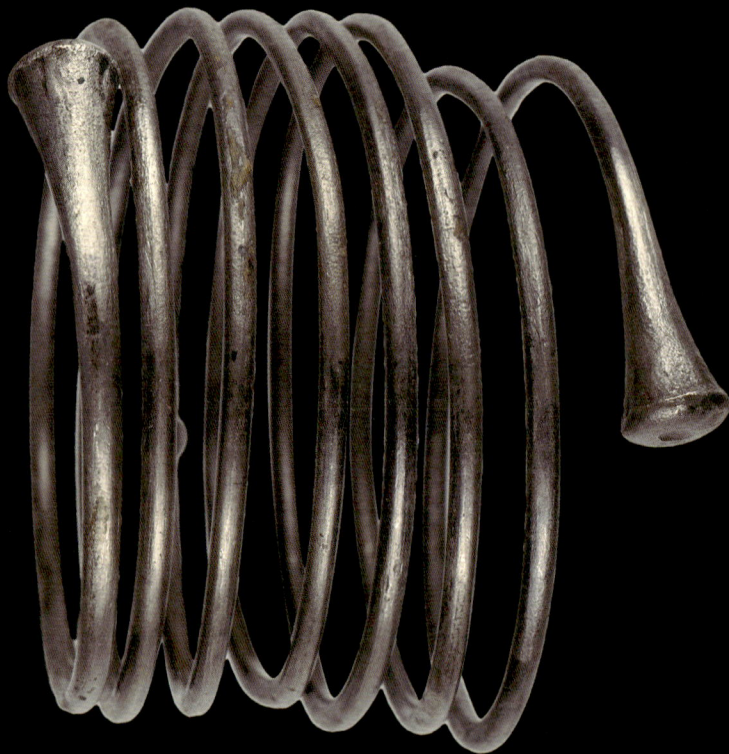

086

一对金臂钏（手镯）

来自爱琴海东北部利姆诺斯岛的波利奥奇发现的"黄金宝藏"

约公元前 2450 — 前 2200 年

Pair of gold armlets (bracelets)

From the "Gold Treasure" found in Poliochni, Lemnos,
NE Aegean Sea
Ca. 2450 – 2200 B.C.
HNAM Π 7171 (2 objects)

这两只手镯均由实心金线制成，缠绕三次，两端呈锥形。在小亚细亚的特洛伊也发现了类似物品。

Both bracelets are made from solid gold wire, wrapped three times and terminating in two conical heads. Similar objects have also been found in Troy, Asia Minor.

087

"8"字盾形黄金吊坠

来自伯罗奔尼撒半岛的皮洛斯

公元前 15 世纪

Gold pendant in the shape of a figure-of-eight shield

From Pylos, Peloponnese
15th century B.C.
HNAM Π 7987

这只吊坠由两片薄金片制成"8"字盾的样式，边缘用黄金造粒工艺加以装饰，且有悬挂孔。

It is made of two thin gold sheets in the shape of a figure-of-eight shield. It bears granulated decorated around the perimeter and has suspension holes.

088

一对金耳饰

来自爱琴海东北部利姆诺斯岛的波利县奇发现的“黄金宝藏”

约公元前 2450 — 前 2200 年

Pair of gold earrings

From the "Gold Treasure" found in Poliochni, Lemnos, NE Aegean Sea

Ca. 2450 – 2200 B.C.

HNAM Π 7186 (2 objects)

　　这对耳饰由两个不同的部分组成：一个实心金丝圆环和一个罂粟花形的吊坠。吊坠上的花苞、花柱甚至花蕊都是用金丝精心制成的。罂粟花的形状和制造技术使这类耳饰在希腊地区独一无二，这也是爱琴海地区最早表现罂粟植物的饰品之一。

　　Gold earrings, composed of two distinct parts: a ring of solid gold wire and the main body in the shape of a poppy flower. The capsule, stamens, and even the pollen are rendered with carefully applied wires. The shape of the poppy flower and manufacturing technique constitute these earrings unique for the region of Greece, while this is one of the earliest representations of the poppy plant in the Aegean area.

089

一对金耳饰

来自爱琴海东北部利姆诺斯岛的波利奥奇发现的"黄金宝藏"

约公元前 2450 — 前 2200 年

Pair of gold earrings

From the "Gold Treasure" found in Poliochni, Lemnos, NE Aegean Sea

Ca. 2450 – 2200 B.C.

HNAM II 7159 (2 objects)

这对耳饰的主体有三排累珠装饰，悬挂着五条装饰有叶子的链条，末端是抽象的人形吊坠。类似的艺术品最早在特洛伊和小亚细亚的其他考古遗址也有发现。这对耳饰发现自一处被称为"波利奥奇宝藏"的考古聚落，可能是因为主人试图贮藏或藏匿而得以保存的。

Three rows of granules decorate the main body from which five chains are suspended decorated with leafs and ending in stylized human-shaped pendants. Comparable artefacts originate from Troy and other archaeological sites in Asia Minor. The presence of the earrings in the so-called "Poliochni Treasure" is possibly related to an attempt to hoard or conceal valuable items.

090

黄金链珠

来自伯罗奔尼撒半岛、迈锡尼、阿西尼、普罗辛那

公元前 14 — 前 13 世纪

浮雕金珠是迈锡尼最受欢迎的珠宝类型，金珠的造型常常模仿花草（如玫瑰、百合、番红花、纸莎草）的形状。

Gold necklaces bead

From Mycenae, Asini, Prosymna, Peloponnese

14th – 13th centuries B.C.

HNAM Π 15794, HNAM Π 15795, HNAM Π 15791,

HNAM Π 2791, HNAM Π 8451β

The gold beads in repoussé decoration became the most popular Mycenaean type of jewellery, often taking forms which imitated flowers (rosettes, lilies, crocus, papyrus).

091

金项链

来自伯罗奔尼撒半岛，迈锡尼的"墓圈B"

公元前 16 世纪

Gold necklace

From Mycenae, Peloponnese, Grave Circle B

16th century B.C.

HNAM Π 8659, HNAM Π 8660 (1 object)

　　这条项链由44颗金片制成的飞鸟形串珠组成。中央的珠子由覆盖陶土芯的金片制成，塑造了一个持"8"形盾牌的勇士，顶部的球形代表勇士的头部。

　　Forty-four beads of gold sheet in the form of schematic birds in flight. The central bead, made of gold sheet over a clay core, depicts a figure-of-eight shield with a spherical top rendering a warrior's head.

这些金片曾包裹在剑鞘上，因此其边缘处留有用于固定的小孔。金片上保留了精致的装饰元素，水平和垂直的分区上均带有浮雕的细小几何图案。

These sheets were once folded around a sword scabbard, hence the tiny holes in the edges for attachment. They preserve elements of an elaborate decoration of vertical and horizontal zones with relief and engraved miniature geometric motifs.

093

黄金饰品

来自伯罗奔尼撒半岛，迈锡尼的"墓圈A"，

3号竖井墓

公元前 16 世纪下半叶

Gold ornament

From Mycenae, Peloponnese, Grave Circle A,

Shaft Grave III

Second half of 16th century B.C.

HNAM Ⅱ 78

这十个迷人的吊坠由薄金片制成，形似昆虫的茧，悬挂在细金链上。

Ten charming pendants made of thin gold sheet, resembling an insect cocoon shape, suspended from fine gold chains.

094

一对金耳环

来自伯罗奔尼撒半岛，迈锡尼的"墓圈 A"

公元前 16 世纪

Pair of gold earrings

From Mycenae, Peloponnese, Grave Circle A

16th century B.C.

HNAM II 55 (2 objects)

这对耳环来自一处被称为"妇女墓"的墓葬。耳环由金线圈制成，末端逐渐变细，形成心形环内的两个优雅螺旋。

Coming from the so-called "Grave of the Women", these earrings made from gold wire becoming thinner towards its ends, forming two elegant spirals inside the heart-shaped loop.

095

一对金耳环

来自伯罗奔尼撒半岛，迈锡尼的"墓圈 A"

公元前 16 世纪

Pair of gold earrings

From Mycenae, Peloponnese, Grave Circle A

16th century B.C.

HNAM II 61 (2 objects)

这对耳环是克里特-迈锡尼珠宝制作的杰出典范，结合了凸纹和黄金造粒工艺。锡拉岛（今圣托里尼岛）阿克罗蒂里壁画中的女性也佩戴着类似的耳环。

Superb example of Creto-mycenean jewellery-making combining repoussé and granulated decoration. Similar earrings are worn by the women in the frescoes from Akrotiri at Thera.

096

金项链

来自伯罗奔尼撒半岛，迈锡尼的"墓圈A"，5号竖井墓

公元前16世纪下半叶

Gold necklace

From Mycenae, Peloponnese, Grave Circle A, Shaft Grave V

Second half of 16th century B.C.

HNAM II 689

　　鹰在古希腊文明中被认为是鸟中之王，代表着力量与尊贵。这条独特的项链属于迈锡尼国王，是他彰显权力和声望的珍贵物品。项链由十个金珠（片）组成，每颗都描绘了一对互为的镜像鹰。

The depiction of the eagle, the king of birds, a symbol of strength and majesty. This unique necklace, a valuable object of power and prestige belonged to a Mycenaean king. It consists of ten beads, each portraying antithetical eagles.

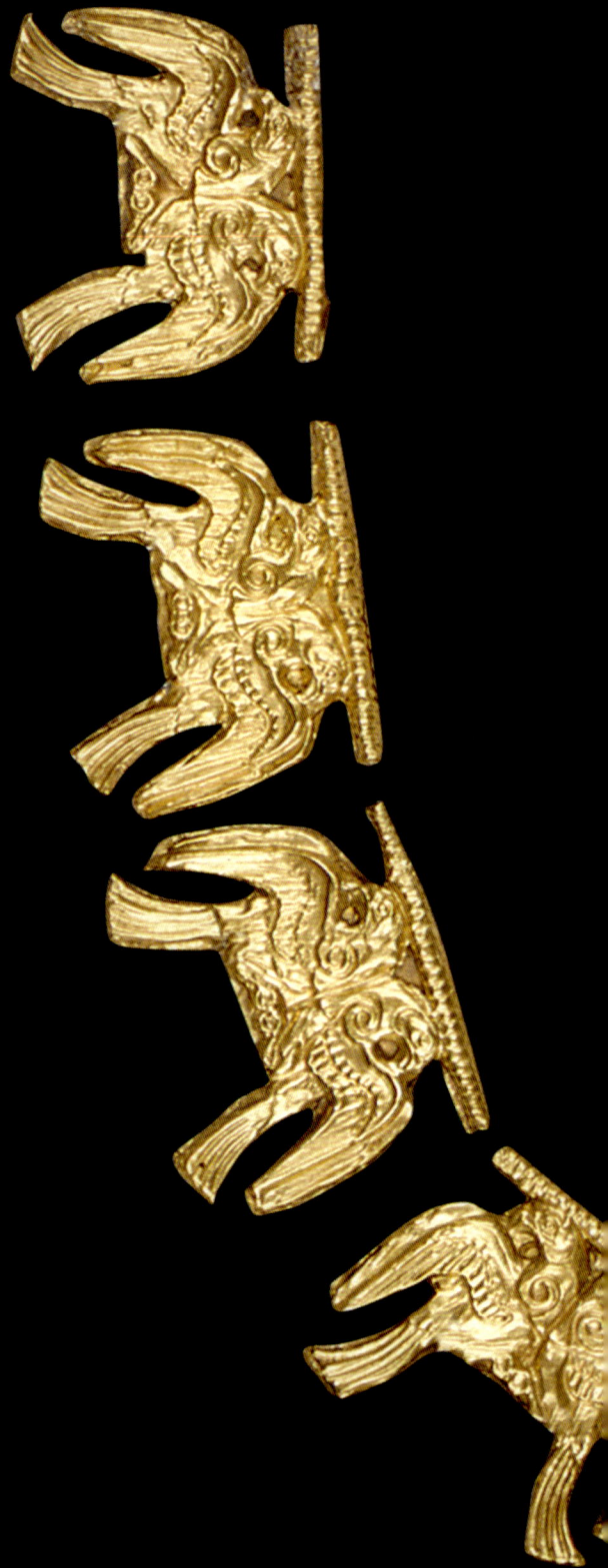

097

黄金项链

来自阿提卡地区的阿纳维索斯公墓

约公元前 800 年

Gold necklace

From Anavyssos cemetery, Attica

Ca. 800 B.C.

HNAM Xρ. 1517

这条编织项链的末端被制成了蛇头形状。编织项链
在公元前 8 世纪成为古希腊女性珠宝的品类之一，可悬
挂在颈部或胸前，并用别衣针或带扣将其末端固定于
肩部。

The woven chain ends in snake heads. The braided chain-
necklace is added to the types of women's ancient Greek jewels in
the 8th century B.C. and adorns either the neck or the chest area
fixed with pins or fibulae on the shoulders.

098

用链子连接的银别衣针

来自克里特岛

公元前 6 — 前 5 世纪

Silver pins connected by a chain

From Crete island

6th – 5th centuries B.C.

HNAM Xρ. 297

这两件固定在衣服上的别衣针的头部呈罂粟荚形，链条末端则是天鹅头形状。

The two pins with heads in the shape of an opium poppy seedpod fastened on to a garment the composite chain ending in swans' heads.

099

金项链

来自阿提卡地区的斯帕塔的墓葬

公元前 725 — 前 700 年

Gold necklace

From a grave in Spata, Attica

725 – 700 B.C.

HNAM Χρ. 1041

这件精致的珠宝由五块小金片以及若干金线、管珠组成，小金片上饰有菱形和月牙形浮雕，图案内部可能曾经镶嵌有宝石或珐琅。

Elaborate jewel of five small plaques, wiry and tubular items with embossed lozenges and crescent-like motifs. Stones or enamel would have been attached to their interior.

IOO

镀金陶土项链   Gilded clay necklace

来源未知   Unknown provenance

公元前 4 世纪中叶   Mid 4th century B.C.

     HNAM Στ. 729

这条由圆盘浮雕和棕榈叶片状装饰物排列而成的项链上，悬挂着陶瓶形状的吊坠，项链以陶土制成，模仿了纯金珠宝的式样。其制作工艺和工艺细节堪称完美，可能来自意大利南部的塔兰托工坊。

From a row of relief discs and palmettes, vase-shaped elements are hanging, in a clay emulation of a real gold jewel. Impeccable artistry and detail, perhaps from a South Italian workshop in Tarent.

101

金项链

来自优卑亚岛（今埃维亚岛）埃雷特里亚的墓葬

公元前 500 — 前 475 年

Gold necklace

From a grave at Eretria, Euboea island

500 – 475 B.C.

HNAM Xρ. 10

这条项链是埃雷特里亚珠宝制作艺术的杰出代表，珠链由橡子形和月桂树果形的精致金珠组成。项链中心装饰着一个牛头形状的吊坠，上面有一对微型女性头像和玫瑰饰纹。项链上的果实和花朵都被塑造得栩栩如生，而牛头在古代象征着能驱除邪祟的力量。

Brilliant example of the Eretrian jewellery-making art composed of intricate beads, elements that take the form of acorns and laurel. The centre is decorated with a pendant in the shape of a bull's head with pairs of tiny female heads and rosettes. The vegetal decoration imitates nature with accuracy. In antiquity the bull was regarded a symbol of power that averted evil.

102

银项链

来自克里特岛

公元前 350 — 前 300 年

Silver necklace

From Crete island

350 – 300 B.C.

HNAM Xρ. 293

这条项链由环形珠子和药膏瓶形状的吊坠组成，较小的吊坠顶部还有玫瑰纹饰。这些瓶形吊坠除了具有装饰作用外，可能还装有药物。

It consists of ring-shaped beads and pendants in the shape of ointment vases. The smaller ones are crowned by rosettes. The decorative vase-like pendants along with their decorative character may have contained pharmaceutical substances.

103

一对金手镯

来源未知（"卡尔派尼西宝藏"）

公元前 3 世纪末 — 前 2 纪初

Gold bracelets

Unknown provenance (from the so – called "Karpenissi Treasure")

Late 3rd – early 2nd centuries B.C.

HNAM Στ. 370, HNAM Στ. 371

　　这对手镯的主体部分由两个用金网覆盖的半圆形金管组成，末端是一个带有浮雕细节的牛头。手镯末端动物头形状的设计具有强烈的东方风格，但可以确定这对手镯是在希腊本土生产的。

They are composed of two semicircular tubes of gold-sheet covered with gold net, ending in a bull-head with embossed details. The animal-like ends recall eastern prototypes, but they were produced by a workshop in the Greek world.

104

黄金项链

来自雅典柏拉图学园的墓葬

公元前 2 世纪

Gold necklace

From a tomb in Plato's Academy, Athens

2nd century B.C.

HNAM Xρ. 1074

　　40颗颜色和形状各异的宝石与黄金串联成了这件奢华的珠宝，遗憾的是，项链中心的吊坠已经遗失。

　　Forty precious stones in various colours and shapes combined with gold, comprise a lavish jewel of which the central pendant is not preserved.

105

黄金项链

来自优卑亚岛（今埃维亚岛）的阿马林索斯的某墓区的坟墓

公元前 2 — 前 1 世纪

Gold necklace

From a grave in a funerary enclosure in Amarynthos, Euboea island

2nd – 1st centuries B.C.

HNAM Xρ. 781

这条项链由球形珠子组成，间隔悬挂着12个尖刺状和心形的装饰物，镶嵌有石榴石、红玉髓和其他宝石，以及一个新月形饰品和一个金质圆柱盒形护身符。类似盒形护身符这样的容器内常发现刻着文字的金属片、织物残片、植物种子、珠子和土壤，有时还有硫黄，它们通常与宗教、魔法或神秘信仰相关。

It consists of globular beads in the interspaces of which hang twelve spiked and heart-shaped items with inset garnets, carnelian and other stones, as well as a crescent-shaped one and a gold cylindrical case-amulet. Inscribed metal sheets, fabric remains, plant seeds, beads, soil, sometimes with sulfur, have been found in cases like this one and they are usually connected with religious, magical or chthonic beliefs.

106

饰有宝石坠和厄洛斯小像的黄金项链

来自塞萨利地区的卡尔季察（"帕拉约卡斯特罗宝藏"）

公元前 1 世纪

Golden necklace with precious stones and a free standing Eros in the middle

From Karditsa (the so – called "Palaiokastron Treasure"), Thessaly

1st century B.C.

HNAM Χρ. 940

镶嵌在这条项链上的彩色宝石与半宝石和厄洛斯小像，将项链装饰得熠熠生辉。

Ornaments with inlaid coloured precious and semi-precious stones and an Eros figure carved in the round compose this impressive necklace.

107

金质带形冠

来自优卑亚岛（今埃维亚岛）阿马林索斯的费利斯科斯之女克莱奥尼凯的墓区内

公元前 2 世纪

Gold ribbon diadem

From the burial enclosure of Kleonike, daughter of Filiskos, in Amarynthos, Euboea island

2nd century B.C.

HNAM Xρ. 767

　　这件被用于葬礼的带形冠，模仿了另一件类似的珍贵首饰的设计，冠上饰有浮雕或镶嵌的半身像，还镶嵌着稀有的紫色玻璃。

　　The embossed decoration of this funerary band diadem is imitating a similar valuable jewel with relief or inlaid busts and glass inlays of rare purple glass.

108

金制吊坠

来自阿提卡地区阿纳维索斯圣潘泰莱蒙的几何陶
时代公墓

公元前 800 — 前 750 年

这件吊坠由一个纵向的圆柱形
柱子和焊接在它两侧的成对螺旋组
成。单个吊坠可用作坠饰，多个则
组合成项链。

Gold pendant

From the Geometric cemetery in Agios
Panteleimon, Anavyssos, Attica

800 – 750 B.C.

HNAM Xρ. 1520

It comprises a lengthwise cylindrical
bead flanked by pairs of spirals soldered
above and below it. This single object
would have served as a pendant (medallion),
while several together would have formed a
necklace.

109

饰有古风时期人物形象的
黄金手镯部件

来自多德卡尼斯群岛的罗得岛

公元前 650 — 前 600 年

Golden plaques forming a bracelet
decorated with Archaic figures

From Rhodes island, Dodecanese

650 – 600 B.C.

HNAM Στ. 241

110

青铜臂钏

来源未知

公元前 8 — 前 7 世纪

由各种工艺制作的单螺旋形或双螺旋形，都是古希腊常见的装饰形状，被运用在扣针、别衣针、手镯、戒指、吊坠等众多类型的珠宝上。

Bronze armlet

Unknown provenance

8th – 7th centuries B.C.

HNAM X 8171

The spiral, simple or double and executed with various techniques, decorated a multitude of ancient jewellery types, such as fibulae, pins, bracelets, finger-rings, pendants.

111

三枚金玫瑰花饰

来自小亚细亚赫勒斯滂地区

公元前 4 世纪

Three gold rosettes

From the Hellespont region, Asia Minor

4th century B.C.

HNAM Στ. 305 (3 objects)

这些花饰由剪裁过的金箔制成，其上有许多精致的雄蕊状装饰，从花朵中心伸展开来，中央的小八叶玫瑰填充有蓝色和白色珐琅。花饰还有着精巧的茎，这表明它们可能曾被固定在诸如腰带等的金属饰板或皮革上，也可能是其他珠宝首饰或装饰品的一部分。

Compound flowers made from cut-out gold sheet, with a multitude of very finely rendered stamens originating from tiny eight-leafed rosettes with blue and white enamel. The occurrence of their elaborate stems indicates that they were probably attached onto a metal plaque or piece of leather, such as a belt, if they were not used as parts of other jewellery or ornaments.

112

金质蛇形手镯

来源未知（"卡尔派尼西宝藏"）

公元前 3 世纪晚期 — 前 2 世纪初

Golden snake bracelets

Unknown provenance (from the so – called "Karpenissi Treasure")

Late 3rd – early 2nd centuries B.C.

HNAM Στ. 346α, β

这对手镯的造型是两条镶嵌着红色半宝石的写实风格的蛇，它们缠绕在女祭司纤细的手臂上，保护她免受一切邪恶力量的侵害。在希腊化时期，手镯和戒指常采用整体蛇形设计。

Two realistically shown snakes, with red semi-precious stones, were wrapped around the delicate arms of a priestess, protecting her from all evil. The bracelet in the form of a full-bodied coiled snake was the paramount type that predominated in the Hellenistic period.

113

一对镶嵌宝石的金手镯

来自塞萨利地区的卡尔季察（"帕拉约卡斯特罗宝藏"）

公元前 1 世纪

Pair of gold bracelets

From Karditsa (from the so – called "Palaiokastron Treasure"), Thessaly

1st century B.C.

HNAM Χρ. 939A, HNAM Χρ. 939B

这是一对工艺精湛的奢华珠宝，饰有镂空叶片和卷须，镶嵌有紫水晶、孔雀石及珐琅。

Luxury jewellery items, of excellent workmanship, with cut-outleaves, tendrils and inset amethysts, malachite stones and enamel.

114

银戒指

来自希腊中部维奥蒂亚塔纳格拉的墓葬

公元前 8 — 前 7 世纪

这是一种在维奥蒂亚女性中很受欢迎的简单首饰，见证了从希腊大陆青铜时代晚期到古风时期金属工艺传统的连续性。

Silver ring

From a tomb at Tanagra, Boeotia, Central Greece

8th – 7th centuries B.C.

HNAM Xρ. 282

Simple jewel of a type popular among ladies in Boeotia, which witnesses the continuity of a long tradition of metalwork from the Late Helladic to the Archaic period.

115

滑石戒指

来自基克拉迪群岛，锡弗诺斯岛

公元前 650 — 前 600 年

这枚罕见的滑石戒指呈淡绿色，戒面描绘了一位手持镜子的蓄须男子。在其座位的高靠背上有一个直立的神灵形象。

Steatite finger ring

From Siphnos, Cyclades

650 – 600 B.C.

HNAM Xρ. 1095

On this rare finger ring made of light green steatite, a bearded man is depicted holding a mirror. An upright demon forms the high back of his seat.

116

金戒指

来自优卑亚岛（今埃维亚岛）的埃雷特里亚

公元前 475 — 前 450 年

戒面上的胜利女神尼姬以高浮雕形式呈现。她穿着长裙，展翅飞翔，手里还持有一串枝丫，可能是月桂枝。

Golden ring

From Eretria, Euboea island

475 – 450 B.C.

HNAM Xρ. 687

On the bezel of the ring, Nike is depicted in high relief, wearing a long dress. She is flying with her wings outspread while holding a laurel (probably) branch.

117

水晶戒指

来自雅典的墓葬

约公元 1 世纪

这是一件极其珍贵和稀有的天然水晶珠宝。它属于为酒神狄俄尼索斯主持神秘祭祀仪式的一位女祭司，此戒指与一系列象征性物品被一同埋葬。

Rock crystal finger ring

From a grave in Athens

1st century A.D.

HNAM A 2774

An extremely valuable and rare rock crystal jewel. It belonged to a priestess of the Dionysiac mysteries, who had been buried with an array of symbolic items.

118

金戒指

来自优卑亚岛（今埃维亚岛）的埃雷特里亚

公元前 475 — 前 450 年

Gold ring

From Eretria, Euboea island

475 – 450 B.C.

HNAM Xρ. 680

戒面用黄金造粒工艺加以装饰并刻有图案。两侧对称的新月形组成了椭圆形的戒面，它们连接在扭转的戒圈上。

Granulated decoration on the bezel and incisions on the ring part. Two juxtaposed elaborate crescents form the bezel while the ring is twisted.

119

镶宝石戒指

来自优卑亚岛（今埃维亚岛）的埃雷特里亚

公元前 5 世纪末

Ring with inset stone

From Eretria, Euboea island

Late 5th century B.C.

HNAM Xρ. 723

这枚金属戒指的戒圈由合金（银与金或其他合金）制成，椭圆形的戒面上镶嵌有红玉髓。宝石上刻有狮身、背部伸出羊头、尾部是一条蛇的喀麦拉图案。戒面边缘饰有绳索图案的浮雕。穿孔的宝石用金线绑在戒圈上。这枚饰有怪物主题浮雕的宝石戒指很可能具有辟邪作用。

Metal ring made of an alloy (silver with gold or other metal alloy) and carnelian in its oval bezel. The stone bears an incised representation of a Chimera with lion body, from the back of which a goat springs out, and a snake tail. Relief cable on the bezel perimeter. The perforated stone is tied to the ring with gold wire. The ring with the invincible monster would probably have had apotropaic character.

120

青铜图章戒指

来源未知

公元前 5 世纪

Bronze signet ring

Unknown provenance

5th century B.C.

HNAM X 26368

这枚戒指的图案灵感可能来源于戏剧。画面中，美狄亚正举起匕首准备杀死自己的孩子们。

The sealing representation of this ring draws inspiration from the theatrical drama and shows Medea lifting the knife to kill her children.

121

刻有胜利女神尼姬的金戒指

来自希腊中部迈索隆吉的克里奥内里的墓葬

公元前 4 世纪

Gold finger ring with an engraved representation of Nike

From a tomb at Kryoneri in Mesologgi, Central Greece

4th century B.C.

HNAM Xρ. 1055α

画面中的人物（胜利女神）正在给一座胜利纪念柱献上桂冠，胜利纪念柱上挂着头盔、盾牌、胸甲和剑。胜利纪念柱是胜利的象征，它由获胜者在战场上树立，上面挂着战败者的武器和盔甲。据推测，这枚戒指的主人可能是战争或爱情中的赢家。

The figure crowns a trophy upon which a helmet, a shield, a breastplate and a sword are set. The trophy, symbol of victory, was a pole erected by the winner in the battle field and upon which the armour of the defeated was placed. The owner of the finger ring would have been victorious in war or in love.

122

镶有厄洛斯金像的玻璃戒指

可能来自克里特岛的斯法基亚

公元前 350 — 前 300 年

Gold-glass finger ring with Eros

Probably from Sphakia, Crete island

350 – 300 B.C.

HNAM Xρ. 2916

厄洛斯倚靠在他的神杖上，正用一只珍贵的浮雕碗饮水，周围是透明的苍穹。

Eros is quenching his thirst by drinking from a valuable relief bowl, leaning on his thyrsus stick and surrounded by the transparent ether.

123

蛇形金戒指

来自优卑亚岛（今埃维亚岛）埃雷特里亚的墓葬

公元前 3 — 前 2 世纪

Gold snake-shaped finger ring

From a grave at Eretria, Euboea island

3rd – 2nd centuries B.C.

HNAM Xρ. 741

这枚戒指也是一件护身符。在希腊化时期，手镯和戒指常采用整体蛇形设计，这可能是受到了与埃及崇拜相关的蛇形保护符号的影响。

Piece of jewellery and at the same time an amulet. During the Hellenistic period bracelets and finger rings took the form of whole-bodied snakes, maybe under the influence of snake-shaped protective symbols related to Egyptian cults.

124

金戒指

来自希腊中部埃托利亚的加瓦洛斯

公元前 200 — 前 150 年

红玉髓戒面上刻有一位缪斯或
迈那得斯，她臀部赤裸，倚靠在一
根柱子上，手持面具和松果酒神杖。
这是一件珍贵的随葬品。

Gold ring

From Gavalos, Aetolia, Central Greece

200 – 150 B.C.

HNAM Xρ. 801

On the carnelian ring-stone, a Muse
or Maenad is depicted with bare buttocks,
leaning on a colonnette and holding a
mask and thyrsos. It was a valuable grave
offering.

125

金戒指

来自优卑亚岛（今埃维亚岛）埃雷特里亚的墓葬

公元前 2 世纪

戒面上刻着爱与美的女神阿佛
洛狄忒。她倚靠在一根柱子上，手
上落有一只鸽子，这是她最喜爱的
象征物之一。

Gold ring

From a grave at Eretria, Euboea island

2nd century B.C.

HNAM Xρ. 612

On the ring-stone is a depiction of
Aphrodite. The goddess of beauty leaning
on a colonnette is holding a dove, one of
her favorite symbols.

126

"Ω"形金耳饰

来自阿提卡地区的莱维迪（坎察）

公元前 725 — 前 700 年

Ω-shaped gold earring

From Levidi (Kantza) Attica

725 – 700 B.C.

HNAM Στ. 297

这是一枚"Ω"形耳环，其末端的锥体塑型极为精准。其象征意义仍不明确。据推测，其佩戴方式应是用细小的圆环悬挂在耳垂上。

A strong Ω-shaped element ends in well-formed cones. The symbolism remains obscure. It would have been suspended from the earlobe by a thin hoop.

127

锥形饰黄金耳饰

来源未知

公元前 8 世纪

Pair of gold earrings with conical finials

Unknown provenance

8th century B.C.

HNAM Στ. 296

128

一对黄金耳环

来自阿提卡地区的阿纳维索斯墓葬

公元前 800 — 前 750 年

Pair of gold earrings

From a grave at Anavyssos, Attica

800 – 750 B.C.

HNAM Χρ. 1519

这对新月形耳环上的镶嵌物已遗失，耳环上悬挂着小巧的编织链。这是受到了东方风格影响的阿提卡作坊的精湛之作。阿提卡的墓葬保留了几何陶时期珠宝艺术的辉煌范例。

Crescent shaped earrings with inlaid, lost today, decoration and small pendent braided chains. Elaborate creation of an attic workshop with oriental influences. Attic cemeteries revealed brilliant examples of jewellery-making art dating in the geometric period.

129

一对黄金耳环

来自阿提卡地区的斯帕塔

公元前 6 世纪末

Pair of gold earrings

From Spata, Attica

Late 6th century B.C.

HNAM Στ. 237

马鸡是一种半马半鸡的神话生物，它正站立在这对耳环的月牙形主体上，这弯新月由细密的金丝和金珠装饰组合而成。

Hippalectryons, half-horse (front) and half-rooster (lower body) mythical creatures, are represented marching atop crescents with rich wire and granulated decoration.

130

金带式耳饰

来自希腊北部的马其顿

公元前 550 — 前 500 年

Pair of gold ribbon earrings

From Macedonia, Northern Greece

550 – 500 B.C.

HNAM Στ. 175

耳环采用金银丝镶嵌和粒状装饰技术。金带可以弯曲形成圆圈，悬挂在细环上作为耳饰。耳环饰有纽索纹和螺旋图案，这是马其顿珠宝艺术的典型类型。

Pair of gold band earrings with guilloche and spiral decoration in filigree and granulation techniques. The bands formed a circle and adorned the female ears hanging from thin rings. Characteristic type of Macedonian jewellery-making art.

131

一对倒锥形金耳饰，上面各站着一位
控制两只狮子的女兽主

来自伯罗奔尼撒半岛，阿尔戈斯城

公元前 650 — 前 625 年

Pair of gold earrings in the shape of
an inverted cone on which stands the
mistress of animals holding two lions from
the legs

From Argos, Peloponnese

650 – 625 B.C.

HNAM Στ. 309α, β

自然的"大女神"将保护佩戴这对耳饰的女性免受
邪恶力量的侵害，作为东方化时期的典型创作，这件珠
宝也强调了女性的美丽。

The Great Goddess of Nature would have protected from the evil
forces the lady who wore them, while at the same time this piece of
jewellery, which was a characteristic creation of the Oriental period,
would have stressed the female beauty.

132

一对金耳饰

来自雅典的克拉美科斯区（陶工区），阿弥莫奈
之女菲洛忒拉之墓

公元 3 世纪

Pair of gold earrings

From the grave of Philotera, daughter of
Amymone, in the Kerameikos, Athens

3rd century A.D.

HNAM Χρ. 78

133

一对金耳饰

来自雅典

公元前 4 — 前 2 世纪

Pair of gold earrings

From Athens

4th – 2nd century B.C.

HNAM Χρ. 15

这对耳环由两只挂着双耳罐形坠饰的精致圆盘构成。

Small amphora (amphoriskoi) are suspended from elaborate discs.

134

一对金耳饰

来自优卑亚岛（今埃维亚岛）的埃雷特里亚

公元前 475 — 前 450 年

Pair of gold earrings

From Eretria, Euboea island

475 – 450 B.C.

HNAM Xρ. 928

这对耳环描绘了海洋女神忒提斯被佛提亚国王珀琉斯掳走的场景。这件独特的艺术品由技艺高超的埃雷特里亚珠宝匠人制作而成，最终陪伴其女主人进入了"永恒的世界"。

The earrings represent the rapture of Nereid Thetis by the king of Phthia Peleus.

The unique work of art, made by a skilled jewel maker from Eretria, followed the lady owner in her eternal home.

135

一对镶嵌宝石的金耳饰

来源未知

公元前 200 — 前 150 年

Pair of gold earrings with precious stones

Provenance unknown

200 – 150 B.C.

HNAM Xρ. 1576

136

一对顶端饰有牛头的环形耳饰

来自塞浦路斯

公元前 4 — 前 2 世纪

Pair of hoop earrings with finials in
the form of bull's head

From Cyprus

4th – 2nd century B.C.

HNAM Xρ. 1147α, β

137

两对黄金耳饰

来自优卑亚岛（今埃维亚岛）的阿马林索斯（克莱奥尼凯 · 菲利斯科之墓）

公元前 2 世纪

Two pairs of gold earrings

From Amarynthos, Euboea island (tomb of Kleonike Philiskou)

2nd century B.C.

HNAM Xρ. 769, HNAM Xρ. 770

　　其中一对耳环用玫瑰花饰来悬挂小型独立的爱神厄洛斯塑像，另一对耳环则用镶嵌有宝石的圆盘来悬挂爱神厄洛斯塑像。

One pair with little free-standing Erotes hanging from rosette and the other with Eros and precious stones.

138

一对金耳饰

来自优卑亚岛（今埃维亚岛）的埃雷特里亚

公元前 150 — 前 100 年

Pair of gold earrings

From Eretria, Euboea island

150 – 100 B.C.

HNAM Xρ. 613

这对耳环采用了金银丝镶嵌技术，并用宝石（石榴石、祖母绿）加以装饰，主体部分则是用圆盘来悬挂鸽子吊饰。

The earrings have decoration in filigree technique and precious stones (garnets, emeralds). The main parts are doves hang from discs.

139

一对镶有图章石的臂环

来自雅典的克拉美科斯区（陶工区），阿弥莫奈之女菲

洛忒拉之墓

公元 3 世纪

Pair of gold armlets with seal stones

From the grave of Philotera, daughter of Amymone,

in the Kerameikos, Athens

3rd century A.D.

HNAM Xρ. 4, HNAM Xρ. 5

臂环上的三块图章石分别描绘了萨尔迪斯的阿尔忒弥斯、以弗所的阿尔忒弥斯和幸运女神堤喀，这表明臂环的主人可能参与了东方的某种宗教仪式。

Three of the seal stones depict Artemis Sardiane, Artemis Ephesia and Tyche Fortuna respectively, suggesting that the owner of the armbands was initiated in Eastern cults.

140

金质护身符（躯干部位的珠宝）

来自优卑亚岛（今埃维亚岛）阿马林索斯的墓葬

公元前 3 — 前 2 世纪

Gold medallion/amulet (piece of jewellery for the torso)

From a grave in Amarynthos, Euboea island

3rd – 2nd centuries B.C.

HNAM Xρ. 768α

这个装饰着半宝石的护身符，可能曾被交叉的链条或皮带类的易腐材料系在墓主人的躯干上，以保护其免受邪恶力量的侵害。这件珍贵的珠宝随她下葬，意在为她提供永恒的守护。

Decorated with semi-precious stones, this amulet was most likely attached to chains or some perishable material and worn crosswise across the torso for protection from evil. This precious ornament followed her to the grave, offering eternal protection.

141

阿提卡黑底红画细颈有柄油瓶

以迈底亚斯瓶画师的风格呈现

来自雅典

公元前 425 — 前 420 年

Attic red-figure lekythos

Rendered in the manner of the Meidias Painter

From Athens

425 – 420 B.C.

HNAM A 13753

　　瓶身画着一位优雅的年轻女子，她佩戴着华丽的珠宝，穿着漂亮的褶裥服装。

　　An elegant young woman, richly decorated with jewellery and nice pleated garment, is represented on the vase.

142

黑底红画双柄细颈高水瓶

来自雅典斯塔迪翁街，皇家马厩的发掘地

公元前 415 — 前 410 年

Red-figure loutrophoros

From Athens, Stadiou Str., excavation of the Royal
Stables

415 – 410 B.C.

HNAM A 16280

瓶身上的画面展示了婚礼前的准备场景。当厄洛斯
来拜访这位新娘时，新娘正要打开箱子，里面放着她的
珠宝和其他能令她更加美丽的秘密。这类容器通常用来
盛装新娘沐浴的水，这时候，新娘会沐浴和涂抹芳香油，
宛如又一个阿佛洛狄忒。

Wedding preparation is displayed. The bride is about to open
the chest in which she keeps her jewels and other secrets of her
beauty, while Eros pays her a visit. This type of vessel was used
to transport water for the bridal bath, and the bride, as another
Aphrodite, would wash and perfume herself.

143

金绞线

来自伯罗奔尼撒半岛，迈锡尼

公元前 14 — 前 13 世纪

Gold twisted wire

From Mycenae, Peloponnese

14th – 13th centuries B.C.

HNAM II 3189

迈锡尼女性会用这种绞线、彩色珠子、丝带和网状
物来装饰她们浓密的秀发。

With twisted wire, colorful beads, ribbons and nets, the
Mycenaean ladies embellished their rich hair.

144

两条金螺旋线（发卷）

来自伯罗奔尼撒半岛的阿西奈

公元前 15 — 前 14 世纪

Two gold spiral wires (hair coils-
sphekoteres)

From Asine, Peloponnese

15th – 14th centuries B.C.

HNAM Π 15867

这两条发卷由坚固的双股金线制成，末端呈环状，
用于固定和装饰单股发丝。

Made of strong double gold wire, the hair coils end in loops and
were used to secure and decorate single strands of hair.

145

金链网头饰

来源未知

公元前 3 — 前 1 世纪

Gold chain-net head jewel

Unknown provenance

3rd – 1st centuries B.C.

HNAM Xρ. 1547

　　在这件头饰中央的圆形装饰上，一名裸体年轻女子正在陶罐旁解开凉鞋，双耳罐中可能装有沐浴用的水。淡蓝色和米白色珐琅装饰着边缘环绕的花环和网链勾连处。

　　The nude young woman on the medallion unfastens her sandal near an amphora, which probably contains water to be used for her bath. A subtle polychromy of light blue and off-white enamel decorates the wreath surrounding the image and the intersections of the net.

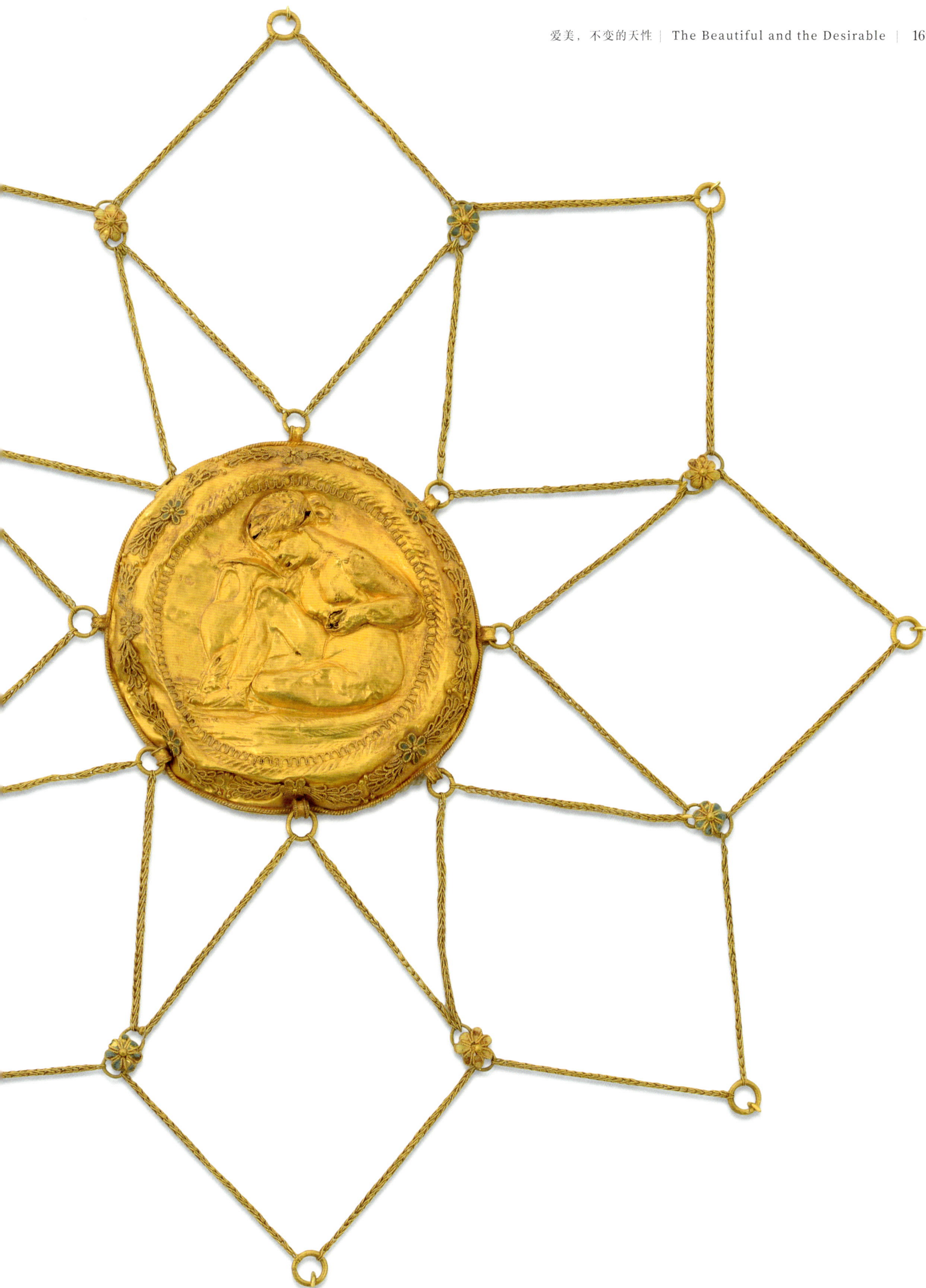

146

金链网头饰

来源未知（"卡尔派尼西宝藏"）

公元前 4 — 前 3 世纪

Gold chain-net head jewel

Unknown provenance (from the so – called "Karpenissi Treasure")

4th – 3rd centuries B.C.

HNAM Στ. 369

这件精致的链网头饰镶嵌有红宝石和蓝珐琅。其中央的圆形装饰上是右肩负着箭筒的女神阿尔忒弥斯像。这件头饰可能曾被用来固定女祭司的发髻。

A fine chain net, adorned with red gems and blue enamel. The goddess Artemis, wearing her arrow case on her right shoulder, is shown on the medallion. It was perhaps made to fasten the gathered up hair of a priestess.

147

女性头像

来自希腊中部，维奥蒂亚的普图翁

公元前 520 — 前 510 年

Head of a female figure

From Ptoon, Boeotia, Central Greece

520 – 510 B.C.

HNAM Γ 17

这尊头像的前额和两鬓排列着整齐的鬈发，耳后的披发呈波浪状，颅顶和枕骨上有纵向的浅凹痕。头发用高高的波浪发冠束住，其上装饰着曲线和算盘图案。耳朵上佩戴着镶有彩色八叶玫瑰的耳环。据推测，这尊头像可能是斯芬克斯或胜利女神尼姬的雕塑。

The elaborated headdress is composed of successive rows of crimped curls on the forehead and temples, wavy curls behind each ear and shallow horizontal grooves on the top and back of the skull. A high, wavy crown, decorated with meander and abacus motif holds back the hair. Round earrings with coloured eight-leaved rosettes adorn the ears. The head belongs probably to a sphinx or a Nike.

148

大理石年轻女性头像

来自伯罗奔尼撒半岛，阿尔戈斯城的赫拉神庙

约公元前 420 年

Marble head of a young woman

From the Argive Heraion, Peloponnese

Ca. 420 B.C.

HNAM Γ 1571

这尊头像的长发用细带束起，垂在颈后。青春的面庞，特别是中分的辫子发型表明她是一位年轻的处女。该头像可能本为神庙建筑装饰的一部分。

The long hair, bound with a fillet, falls over the nape. The soft facial skin and especially the braid along the central parting characterize her as a young virgin. It probably belonged to the architectural decoration of the temple.

149

戏剧面具式大理石女性头像

来源未知

公元 1 世纪末

Marble female head in the form of a
theatrical mask

Unknown provenance

End of the 1st century A.D.

HNAM Γ 505

　　女性浓密的卷发围绕着脸部结成发绺。其皮肤经过
了抛光处理。浮雕的眉毛被着色突出。眼睛是镶嵌的，
带有可能由玻璃制成的虹膜。

　　The woman's hair forms a toupet around the face, which
is made up of thick tight curls. The skin is polished. The relief
eyebrows are highlighted in color. The eyes were inlaid. The irises
were probably made of glass.

PERFUME 香
氛

当人类将香气与美丽结合在一起的时候，使用芳香油的历史也就开始了。在迈锡尼时期，芳香油生产是最繁荣的王室产业之一。

线性文字B泥板为我们留下了许多关于迈锡尼时期生活方式的历史线索，其中就有以橄榄油为底油的芳香油的宝贵信息。这些芳香油呈液体或半流质形式，用莎草、鼠尾草、芫荽和玫瑰等植物和草药调香。尽管这些芳香油确切的生产方式尚不清楚，但毫无疑问必须经过熬煮制造。

The use of perfumed oils can be traced back in the history of mankind connecting fragrance with beauty. During the Mycenaean period perfume production was one of the most flourishing palatial industries.

The written evidence from the Linear B tablets includes valuable information about olive-oil based perfumes in fluid or thick liquid form, scented with plants and herbs such as cyperus, sage, coriander and rose. Though the exact manufacturing process is not known, there is no doubt that it included boiling.

150

线形文字 B 泥板

来自伯罗奔尼撒半岛迈锡尼时代皮洛斯的王宫
公元前 13 世纪末期

泥板上记录着由莎草和玫瑰花瓣调制的芳香油的库藏情况。

Linear B tablet

From the Mycenaean palace at Pylos, Peloponnese
End of the 13th century B.C.
HNAM II 24049, PY Fr 1203

The tablet records stored oil, perfumed with cyperus and rose petals.

151

线形文字 B 泥板

来自伯罗奔尼撒半岛，迈锡尼时代皮洛斯的王宫

公元前 13 世纪末期

Linear B tablet

From the Mycenaean palace at Pylos, Peloponnese

End of the 13th century B.C.

HNAM Π 23674, PY Un 592

　　泥板上，宫廷书记员记录了芫荽、羊毛、"果实"以及其他交给香水制造商制作芳香油的原料。

The palatial scribe records on this tablet coriander, wool, "fruit", along with other ingredients handed over to the perfume makers to produce perfumed oil.

152

线形文字 B 泥板

来自伯罗奔尼撒半岛，迈锡尼时代皮洛斯的王宫

公元前 13 世纪末期

Linear B tablet

From the Mycenaean palace at Pylos, Peloponnese

End of the 13th century B.C.

HNAM Π 12589, PY Un 616 (recto)

泥板三面都有字。正面记录了大量莎草（1296升）、芫荽和坚果的明细。这些植物可能在当时有很多用途，而在这块泥板上，它们是作为迈锡尼时代王宫繁荣的香水工业原材料被记录下来的。

This tablet is written on its three sides. The front side recto records a large quantity of cyperus (1296 litres) along with coriander and possibly nuts. Although these plants may have been used in various ways, they are included in the tablet as raw materials for the flourishing perfume industry of the Mycenaean palaces.

153

微型金圆盒

来自伯罗奔尼撒半岛，迈锡尼的"墓圈 A"

公元前 16 世纪

Miniature gold pyxis

From Mycenae, Peloponnese, Grave Circle A

16th century B.C.

HNAM II 85

这个小巧、紧闭的金盒被用来盛装一种珍贵的固体物质，这种固体物质可能是在涂香或芳香理疗时使用的，必须密封以保持其特质。

This small, tightly covered, gold box was meant to contain a precious solid substance, possibly aromatic–pharmaceutical, which had to be stored airtight, in order to maintain its properties.

154

线形文字 B 泥板

来自伯罗奔尼撒半岛，迈锡尼时代皮洛斯的王宫

公元前 13 世纪末期

Linear B tablet

From the Mycenaean palace at Pylos, Peloponnese

End of the 13th century B.C.

HNAM Ⅱ 24035, PY Fr 1184

　　根据泥板记录，香水制造商科卡洛斯向他的同行尤米德斯交付了 38 个装满 518.4 升香水的大型商用陶罐。芳香油和香膏可用于化妆和治疗，可能还有一定的仪式用途。

　　The tablet records the perfume maker Kokalos who delivers to his colleague Eumedes 38 large stirrup jars filled with 518.4 litres of perfumed oils. Perfumed oils and unguents had cosmetic, pharmaceutical and possibly ceremonial uses.

155

线形文字 B 泥板

来自伯罗奔尼撒半岛，迈锡尼的"狮身人面像之宅"

公元前 13 世纪末期

Linear B tablet

From the "House of the Sphinxes" at Mycenae, Peloponnese

End of the 13th century B.C.

HNAM Π 7704, MY Ge 606

　　泥板上记录的某些植物，如番红花、芫荽、茴香、黄连木、芝麻和薄荷，可能是用于生产芳香油的原材料。

Certain plants recorded in the tablet such as safflower, coriander, fennel, terebinth, sesame and mint might have been used as raw materials to produce perfumed oil.

156

线形文字 B 泥板

来自伯罗奔尼撒半岛，迈锡尼时代皮洛斯的王宫

公元前 13 世纪末期

Linear B tablet

From the Mycenaean palace at Pylos, Peloponnese

End of the 13th century B.C.

HNAM Π 12573, PY Vn 130

根据泥板记录，凯桑德罗丝负责监督皮洛斯王国不
同地区的芳香油制作工作，尤其是容器的生产和煮沸香
料所必需的木材的采买。

According to the tablet, Kessandros supervises perfume
making operations in different areas of the Pylian kingdom and
especially the production of container vases and the procurement
of timber which was essential for the boiling of perfumes.

157

线形文字 B 泥板

来自伯罗奔尼撒半岛，迈锡尼的"油商之宅"

公元前 13 世纪末期

Linear B tablet

From the "House of the Oil Merchant" at
Mycenae, Peloponnese
End of the 13th century B.C.
HNAM Π 7767, MY Fo 101

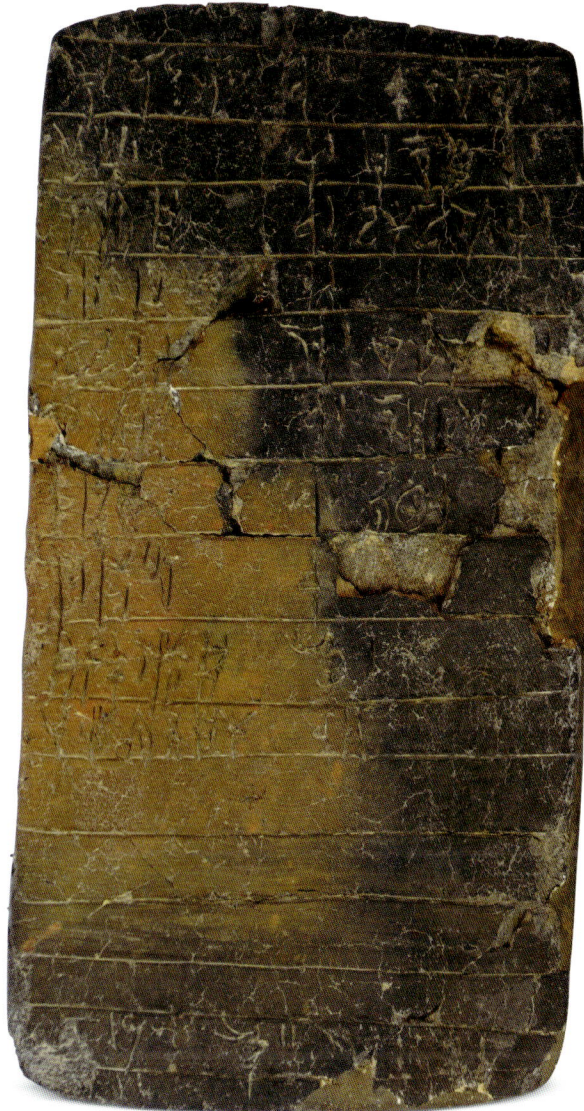

这块泥板上记录了给从事纺织工作的女工分发加工过的芳香油的情况。在这种情况下，芳香油可能被用来对线进行清洁、软化和增添香味。

The tablet records the distribution of processed oil to groups of craftswomen involved in the cloth industry. In this case, the perfumed oil was probably used to clean, soften and scent the threads.

158

马镫柄罐

来自阿提卡地区的马尔科普洛

公元前 13 世纪

Stirrup jars

From Markopoulo, Attica

13th century B.C.

HNAM Π 3892, HNAM Π 3898, HNAM Π 3894,

HNAM Π 3889, HNAM Π 3897

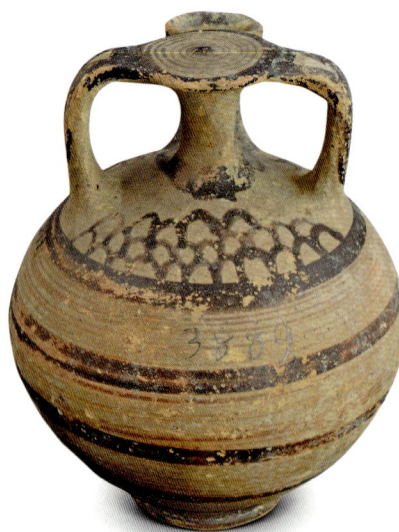

马镫柄罐在迈锡尼时期被广泛用于对芳香油的存储和运输，在定居点和墓葬中多有发现。罐身上的彩绘装饰多采用别具风格的花朵图案，让人联想起制作芳香油时所用的芳香植物。

Stirrup jars were the most popular vessels for the storage and transportation of perfumed oil during the Mycenaean period and are common finds in both settlements and burials. Their painted decoration, often showing stylized flowers, may be evoking the aromatic plants used as ingredients in the production of perfumed oil.

159

有滤孔的陶炉（香炉）

来自基克拉迪群岛，锡拉岛（今圣托里尼岛）的

阿克罗蒂里

公元前 16 世纪

Clay perforated strainer pyraunon
(incense burner)

From Akrotiri, Thera, Cyclades

16th century B.C.

HNAM Π 27473 [AKP 1169]

　　在特殊容器中燃烧芳香油和香料是熏香和为空间消
毒时的常见做法，偶尔也用于宗教仪式与宴席。

　　Burning perfumed oils and incense in special vessels was a
common practice for perfuming and disinfecting space, occasionaly
as an offer of religious character, but also during feasts.

160

迈锡尼马镫柄罐

来自埃及，罗斯托维奇收藏

新王国时期，公元前 1550 — 前 1307 年

Mycenaean stirrup jars

From Egypt, Rostovitch collection

New Kingdom, 1550 – 1307 B.C.

HNAM AIΓ 6851α, HNAM AIΓ 6851β (2 objects)

在东地中海地区广泛发现的马镫柄罐证明了迈锡尼芳香油在当时具有商业价值，也解释了迈锡尼王室为何如此重视其生产。

Stirrup jars have come to light throughout the Eastern Mediterranean, demonstrating the commercial value of the Mycenaean perfumed oils, thus explaining the care showed by the Mycenaean palaces for monitoring their production.

161

早期基克拉迪文化罕见的留有镀银残迹的陶罐

来自基克拉迪群岛，纳克索斯的斯佩多斯墓葬

早期基克拉迪文化二期，公元前 2800 — 前 2300 年

Rare early Cycladic jug with traces of silver
plating

From Spedos cemetery at Naxos, Cyclades

Early Cycladic II period, 2800 – 2300 B.C.

HNAM II 6109.1

　　经化学分析证实，陶罐里盛放的物质是橄榄油。这
表明早在公元前三千纪，爱琴海地区就开始种植橄榄
树了。

Chemical analysis has shown that the juglet contained olive oil.
This is an indication that olive trees were cultivated in the Aegean as
early as the 3rd millennium B.C.

古代的香水
PERFUMES IN ANTIQUITY

古代一些著名的香水，包括鸢尾花香水（由鸢尾花和百合花制成）、玫瑰油膏（用玫瑰花瓣调制而成）、桃金娘香水（从阿佛洛狄忒的圣树桃金娘的叶子和橡子中提取原料）。彼时流行的香氛还包括由草药和树脂混合制成的芳香油，例如从缬草中提取的缬草芳香油，从东方进口的灌木没药树或没药中提取的没药树脂芳香油，从同名开花植物中提取的香脂芳香油，以及因其香甜柔和的香气而闻名的、由胡芦巴种子制成的胡芦巴芳香油。

古代文献中记录了各种香水和药膏的详细资料，包括它们的成分和炮制方法。其中较为突出的是第奥斯库里德斯的精细配方和赛奥法拉斯托斯的手札，这些文献为再现古代的香水实验提供了可能和宝贵的指导。

Some of the renowned perfumes in antiquity were the irinon made out of irises and lilies, the rodion myron, an unguent of rose petals, and the myrtinon myron, extracted from the leaves and acorns of myrtle, the sacred plant of Aphrodite. Popular fragrances were also concocted from herbs and gum resins, such as the nardion or nardinon myron, from the valerian plant, the stakti, a myrrh gum essential oil from the shrub Commiphora myrrha or smyrna, imported from the East, the balsamon from the similarly called flowering plant, and the tilinon oil, famous for its sweet and soft fragrance, made from the seeds of fenugreek.

Ancient sources record details about the various kinds of perfumes and ointments, their ingredients and methods of manufacture. Standing out among them are Dioskurides' elaborate recipes and Theophrastus' texts, which served as a valuable guide for the experimental creation of the perfumes.

162

大理石阿佛洛狄忒小雕像

来自雅典的忒修斯神庙区域

公元前 1 世纪

Marble statuette of Aphrodite

From the area of Theseion, Athens

1st century B.C.

HNAM Γ 2585

女神身体前倾，极富动感地向前迈出左腿，同时上身转向相反方向。透明而精致的长裙（希顿）高束在其胸部以下，展现出她丰满的身体曲线。她的披肩（希玛纯）垂下，紧紧覆盖在其大腿上。

The goddess moves forward, advancing dynamically the left leg, while bending the torso to the opposite direction. The fine, transparent chiton, girt high beneath the breast reveals the rich curves of her body. The himation is wrapped around her thighs.

163

大理石阿佛洛狄忒小雕像

来自伯罗奔尼撒半岛，阿尔戈斯城

公元前 1 世纪

Marble statuette of Aphrodite

From Argos, Peloponnese

1st century B.C.

HNAM Γ 3248

　　雕像的右脚坚实地踏在椭圆形基座上，左腿则向前弯曲，脚轻点在一只鹅上。她只穿着一件袒露胸部的披肩（希玛纯），躯干因她的姿态而富有强烈的动感。

The figure steps firmly with the right foot on the ellipsoidal plinth, while she leans the left leg, bent forward, on a goose. She wears only a himation that leaves the breast exposed. The movement of the torso is strongly antithetical.

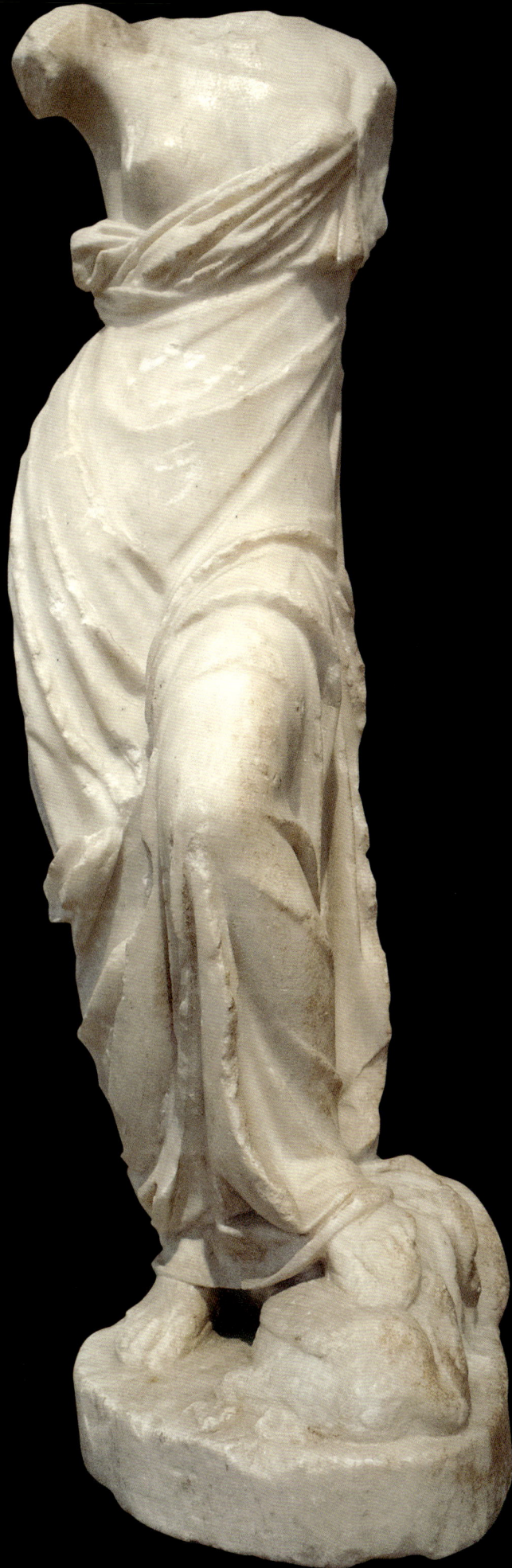

164

森托切勒式大理石厄洛斯小雕像

来自伯罗奔尼撒的埃庇道鲁斯

公元 3 世纪初

Marble statuette of Eros in the Centocelle type

From Epidaurus, Peloponnese

Early 3rd century A.D.

HNAM Γ 5245

这个裸体少年雕像的肩膀后面有两个用于插入金属翅膀的孔，因此其被认定为阿佛洛狄忒的儿子厄洛斯。许多学者认为这种雕塑类型的原创者为普拉克西特列斯。

The statuette of the nude adolescent bears two holes at the back of the shoulders for inserting metal wings, leading to its identification with Eros, Aphrodite's son. The original of the statuary type has been attributed by many scholars to Praxiteles.

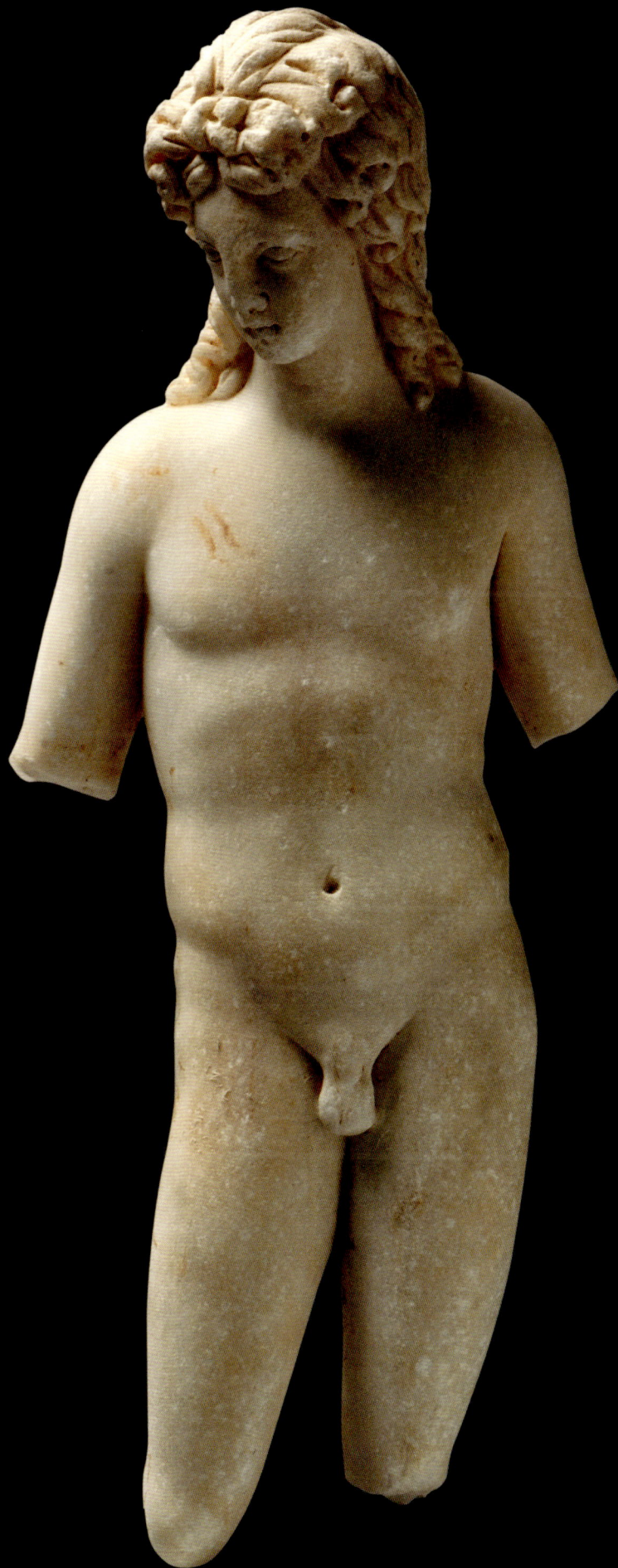

3

SECTION III .

FOCUSING ON THE BODY

镌美，卓越的塑造

从史前时期开始，人体及其细节就用各种材料和形式被表现出来。在所有文化中，人们都努力将对自身及其在世界中的位置的体验和感知融入艺术表达。

在希腊大陆的史前社会，身体特征被视为信仰的标志，与自然紧密相连。新石器时代，以裸体丰满女性形象为主题的艺术创作广泛地以石头和陶土作为媒介表现。与此同时，基克拉迪文化则发展出一种对裸体女性和男性进行抽象表现的大理石雕塑。类似具有象征性的形象在米诺斯、锡拉岛和迈锡尼文明的各类艺术品中也不鲜见，女性多身材丰腴，穿着衣物但袒露乳房，而男性多为穿着衣物或穿着独特缠腰布半裸的形象。

在历史的长河中，社会和政治条件逐渐塑造了人们对人的价值和潜力的新认识。几何陶时期的青铜雕像反映了这个英雄时代的精神。在古风时期，社会需求导致了大型雕塑的诞生，雕塑的主要题材为健壮的裸体青年以及盛装的优雅少女，直到古典时期，平衡、对称与和谐的原则盛行。雕塑作品体现了永恒的美丽和青春、内在和外在的均衡发展。在希腊化时期，雕塑偏好表达写实的剧烈动作和迸发的激情，而从公元前2世纪末开始直至整个罗马时期，艺术又回到古典时期的作品范例中汲取灵感和指引。

Right from the earliest days of prehistory, the body and its details are depicted in various materials and forms. In all cultures, an effort is made to enclose into its rendering the experiences and the perceptions man construes in relation to himself and his position in the world.

In the prehistoric societies of the helladic area, the body features as a symbol of beliefs, closely linked with nature. In the Neolithic period, nude women with fuller figures prevail in stone and clay, while emerging from the Cycladic culture is an abstract type of marble nude female and male figurines. Similar emblematic images are encountered in the diverse works of the Minoan, Theran and Mycenaean world, which represent the women dressed, with voluminous and often bare breasts, and the men dressed or semi-nude bearing the characteristic loincloth.

In the course of the historic times, social and political conditions shaped gradually a new perception of the value and potential of man. The bronze figurines of the Geometric period reflect the spirit of this heroic era. In Archaic times, inquisitions lead to the birth of large-scale sculpture with the robust bodies of nude youths (kouroi) and dressed graceful maidens (korai), until in Classical times, the principles of balance (metron), symmetry and harmony prevail. Sculpted works of art embody the timeless beauty and youthfulness, the even development of mind and form. There follows realism in the depiction of the body, with the strong movements and the explosive passion of the Hellenistic times, while from the end of the 2nd century B.C. and throughout the Roman times art often draws inspiration and guidance from the Classical prototypes.

165

女祭司和其他女性石雕小像

来自伯罗奔尼撒半岛，斯巴达

新石器时代早期，公元前 6500 — 前 5800 年

Stone figurines of a priestess and other female figures

From Sparta, Peloponnese

Early Neolithic period, 6500 – 5800 B.C.

HNAM Π 3931, HNAM Π 3930, HNAM Π 3929, HNAM Π 3928

裸体的"女祭司"头戴特色头饰，肩膀上有锯齿形
和菱形的刻痕符号，伴之以三个更加简化的女性形象。
它们被发现时周围还伴有绿色石珠和小型白石容器，很
可能展现了新石器时代某种仪式的场景。

The nude "priestess" with the characteristic head cover and
the incised symbols of zig-zag and lozenges on the shoulders, is
accompanied by three more schematic female figures. They were
found together with beads of green stone and small vessels of white
stone, revealing an aspect of Neolithic ritual.

166

"思考者"陶俑

来自塞萨利地区的卡尔季察

新石器时代晚期，公元前 4500 — 前 3300 年

Clay figure of a "thinker"

From Karditsa, Thessaly

Final Neolithic period, 4500 – 3300 B.C.

HNAM II 5894

这名男子正用右手扶头做出沉思的姿态，同时也展现着他的男性生殖力。围绕其裸露的颈部和腹股沟处刻有网状图案。在新石器时代的仪式中，这件大型雕像会被众人观摩。在当时，只有男性形象会被描绘为"思考者"，尤其是在巴尔干地区。

The man brings his right hand to his head in a gesture of pondering, while also stimulating the generative power of his manhood. On his nude body, incised net surrounds the neck and the groin. In Neolithic rituals, this large-sized figure would have been visible to a crowd of people. Only male figures are depicted as "thinkers", especially in the Balkans.

167

大理石裸体女性小雕像

来自基克拉迪群岛纳克索斯岛的斯佩多斯

早期基克拉迪文化二期

公元前 2800 — 前 2300 年

Marble nude female figurine

From Spedos, Naxos, Cyclades

Early Cycladic II period

2800 – 2300 B.C.

HNAM Π 6140.22

这个身材高挑、纤细的女性小雕像，拥有少女般小巧的胸部和曲线优美的长腿，完美地表达了早期基克拉迪文化鼎盛时期雕塑家的审美理想。曾经被涂上颜色的眼睛让这位女性的面部更加生动。

This tall and slender figurine with her small, youthful breasts and curved thighs expresses properly the aesthetic ideal of the sculptors in the peak of the Cycladic civilization. The once painted eyes were livening up the face of the woman.

168

大理石小雕像

来自基克拉迪群岛的纳克索斯岛

早期基克拉迪文化一至二期

公元前 2800/ 公元前 2700 年

Marble figurine

From Naxos, Cyclades

Early Cycladic I – II

2800/2700 B.C.

HNAM Π 6140.7

这一高度抽象的人体形象带有鲜明的纳克索斯岛风格，表明它是当地的产物。它与一组类似的小雕像在一个豪华的墓葬中被一同发现。大理石小雕像是尊贵之物，陪伴当时社会的显要人物入葬，被认为是神祇、灵魂的象征或死者的仆人。

Highly schematized human figure, easily identifiable as Naxian and therefore indicative of localized production. It was found together with a group of similar figurines in a richly furnished burial. Marble figurines are objects of prestige, accompany prominent members of society in the grave and have been interpreted as deities, depictions of the soul or servants of the dead.

169

一对女性和男性的铅制小雕像

来自伯罗奔尼撒半岛，美塞尼亚的坎波斯

公元前 15 世纪

Pair of lead figurines, female and male

From Kambos, Messenia, Peloponnese

15th century B.C.

HNAM Π 3301, HNAM Π 3302

这些具有米诺斯风格的小雕像将克里特社会对男性
和女性的理想形象传播到了希腊大陆。

These are Minoan type figurines transmitting to the Greek
mainland the ideal of the Cretan society for the representation of
male and female figures.

170

金质图章戒指

来自伯罗奔尼撒半岛，迈锡尼
公元前 15 世纪

Gold signet rings

From Mycenae, Peloponnese
15th century B.C.
HNAM Π 3148, HNAM Π 992

　　戒面展示的仪式场景中，男性通常被描绘为半裸形象，穿着用腰带束紧的短衣，而女性则有丰满的胸部，穿着长褶裙。

　　In ritual scenes men are usually depicted semi-nude, with a short garment tightly held with a belt, while women have prominent breasts and wear long pleated skirts.

171

黄金刻像

来自伯罗奔尼撒半岛，迈锡尼，"墓圈 A"
公元前 16 世纪

Gold cut out

From Mycenae, Peloponnese, Grave Circle A
16th century B.C.
HNAM Π 27

　　这件作品中完全裸露的女性身体、其突出的三角形耻骨以及整体审美品位应是源自东方，在米诺斯人和迈锡尼人的作品中并不常见。而她放在胸前的手臂和头顶上的鸟可能具有某种宗教意义。

　　The total nudity of the female body with accentuated pubic triangle and the overall aesthetic approach were not common to the Minoans and Mycenaeans, as they originate from eastern prototypes. The position of the arms on the breasts and the bird on top of the head probably bear religious significance.

172

女性队伍场景的壁画残片

来自伯罗奔尼撒半岛，梯林斯卫城

公元前 13 世纪

Fresco fragment from a women's procession scene

From the Tiryns acropolis, Peloponnese

13th century B.C.

HNAM Π 5883α

这是一幅曾装饰在梯林斯宫殿内的壁画，展现了一队妇女向神祇或迈锡尼统治者进献珍贵礼物的画面。这些妇女可能是女神或者上流社会的女性，她们精致的发型和华服下丰满的乳房令人印象深刻。

A procession of women offering valuable gifts towards a deity or towards the Mycenaean ruler, once decorated the walls of the Tiryns palace. These women, either divine beings or ladies of status, are impressive with their elaborate hair styling and their ample bosom accentuated by their luxurious dress.

173

显圣的宙斯青铜小雕像

来自伯罗奔尼撒半岛，奥林匹亚圣地

公元前 10 世纪末 — 前 8 世纪初

Bronze figurines of Zeus in the divine epiphany

From the sanctuary of Olympia, Peloponnese

End of 10th – beginning of 8th centuries B.C.

HNAM X 6168, HNAM X 6093, HNAM X 6108, HNAM X 6167

各种神祇，特别是宙斯形象的小雕像是奥林匹亚圣
地珍贵的祭品。在最早期的雕像中，宙斯总是伸出或举
起手臂，显示其神力。上图中第一件青铜宙斯像躯干较
短，身体的主要部分在空中伸展并被拉长。

Figurines of various deities, especially Zeus, were precious
votive offerings at the Sanctuary of Olympia. In the earliest of them,
Zeus is rendered with extended or upraised arms, declaring his
divine appearance (epiphany). The torso is short and the main parts
of the body are elongated and outstretched in space.

174

裸体女性青铜小雕像

来源未知
公元前 9 世纪

Bronze nude female figurine

Unknown provenance
9th century B.C.
HNAM X 15150

这座雕像实际上是二维的，在高度和宽度上进行了延伸。其着重描绘了连续的轮廓和人体的结构特征。

The figure is in fact two dimensional, extending in height and width. Emphasis is given to the continuous outline and depiction of the anatomical features.

175

裸体女性青铜小雕像，可能来自某容器的装饰

来自雅典 卫城
公元前 8 世纪晚期

Bronze nude female figurine, possibly from the decoration of a vessel

From the Acropolis, Athens
Late 8th century B.C.
HNAM X 6503

可以从这座雕像中辨认出能确定女性性别的身体解剖特征。这座雕像是基于垂直和水平轴塑造的，保持着正面造型。卫城圣地的祭品中有许多都是代表运动员、男女青年或其他人物的小雕像。

The anatomical features of the body for the declaration of the female gender can be discerned. The figure is shaped on the basis of the vertical and horizontal axes, still maintaining the frontal position. Numerous male and female figurines representing athletes, youths (kouroi) and maidens (korai), and other figures, were votive offerings in the sanctuary of the Acropolis.

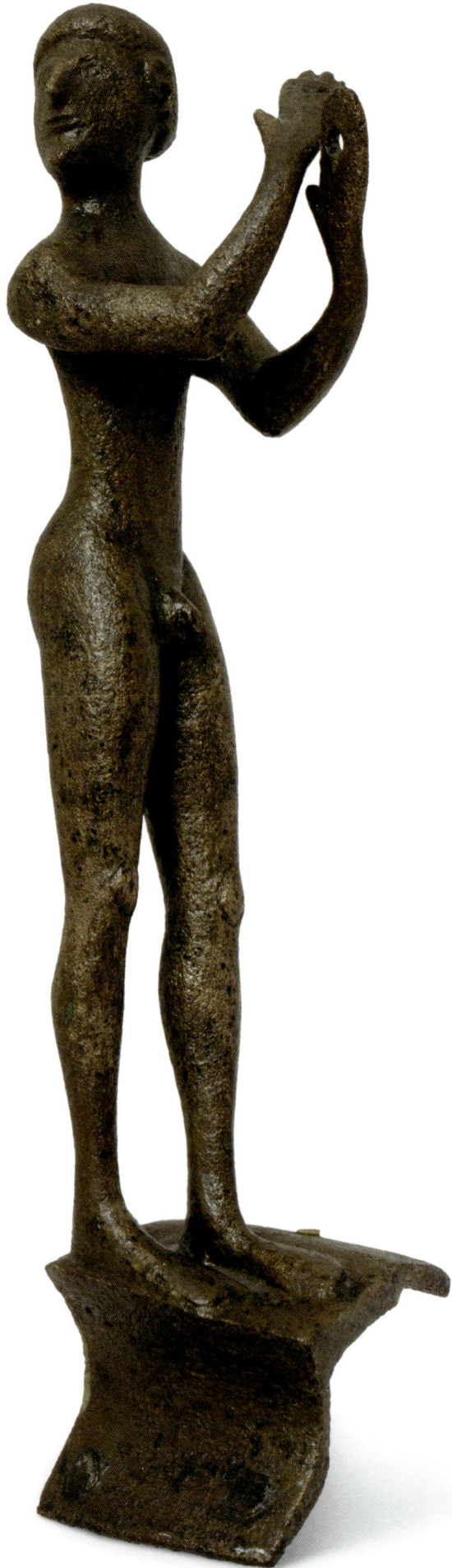

176

青铜裸体男性小雕像

来自伯罗奔尼撒半岛，奥林匹亚圣地

公元前 750 — 前 725 年

Bronze nude male figurine

From the Sanctuary of Olympia, Peloponnese

750 – 725 B.C.

HNAM X 6179

　　这个雕像曾被装饰在三足锅的把手上。其面部特征、躯干和腿部的纤细比例，以及头部、双手和左脚的动作显示出晚期几何陶时期艺术中雕像结构的先进性，但同时也能看到其姿势被塑造得有些僵硬。

The figure adorned the handle of a tripod cauldron. The features of the face, the slender proportions of the torso and the legs, the movement of the head, the hands and the left foot show an advanced structuring of the figure in the art of the Late Geometric period and at the same time indicate the distancing from the stiff posture of the body.

177

青铜勇士小雕像

来自伯罗奔尼撒半岛，奥林匹亚圣地

公元前 8 世纪中叶

Bronze figurine of a warrior

From the Sanctuary of Olympia, Peloponnese

Mid 8th century B.C.

HNAM X 6178

这名勇士戴着尖顶头盔，具有几何陶时期陶瓶绘画中类似形象的特征——细长的双腿、菱形的躯干、三角形的头部和突出的下巴。裸体男性、勇士和马车手的小雕像，以及装饰三足锅的马匹小雕像都是那个时代圣地最珍贵的供品。

The male figurine wears a crested helmet. Slender legs, a rhomboid torso, triangular head shape with accentuated chin, are features of similar figures in vase painting of the Geometric period. Figurines of nude male figures, warriors, charioteers as well as horses adorned the handles of tripod cauldrons, the most precious votive offerings in the sanctuaries of that era.

178

青铜勇士小雕像

来自伯罗奔尼撒半岛，奥林匹亚宙斯圣地

公元前 7 世纪初

Bronze figurine of a warrior

From the Sanctuary of Zeus at Olympia, Peloponnese

Early 7th century B.C.

HNAM X 6178α

这名勇士佩戴着有装饰的头盔和宽腰带，右手可能曾握有长矛，左手持盾牌。该雕像描绘的可能是勇士形象的宙斯。

The male figurine wears a crested helmet and a wide waistband. In the right hand he probably held a spear, in the left one a shield. It is possibly a representation of Zeus as warrior.

179

青铜勇士小雕像

来自塞萨利地区的卡尔季察

约公元前 700 年

Bronze statuette of a warrior

From Karditsa, Thessaly

Ca. 700 B.C.

HNAM X 12831

这名勇士佩戴着一顶早期的圆锥形头盔、一条多层圆环构成的腰带，以及一面悬挂在背后肩带上的维奥蒂亚式"8"形盾牌。其颈部、生殖器和小腿被突出刻画，展现出男性的强健体魄和无畏的战斗精神，很可能代表了勇敢的英雄阿喀琉斯。

The male figurine wears an early type of conical helmet, a waistband, indicated by multi plerings, and has a figure-eight shield of Boeotian type, hanging from the baldric on his back. The neck, the genitals and the shins are excessively stressed, exposing the robust male body and the strength of an outstanding warrior, who most probably represents the brave hero Achilles.

180

青铜库罗斯（男青年）小雕像

来自伯罗奔尼撒半岛，巴赛的阿波罗 · 伊壁鸠鲁神庙

公元前 550 — 前 500 年

Bronze kouros figurine

From the Sanctuary of Apollo Epikourios at Bassae, Peloponnese

550 – 500 B.C.

HNAM X 13685

这尊雕像可能是阿波罗的形象。雕像描绘了男性身体的结构特征并勾勒出肌肉线条。

It is possibly a representation of Apollo. The anatomical features are depicted as well as an attempt to delineate the body musculature.

181

大理石库罗斯（阿波罗或男青年）雕像

来自希腊中部，维奥蒂亚普图翁的阿波罗圣地

约公元前 520 年

Marble statue of a kouros (Apollo/youth)

From the Apollo sanctuary in Ptoon, Boeotia, Central Greece

Ca. 520 B.C.

HNAM Γ 12

库罗斯（男青年）是古风时期艺术（公元前 7 世纪—前 6 世纪）中最重要的一种雕塑类型，体现了当时的贵族阶层理想的状态。库罗斯要么描绘神祇，要么描绘最具美貌和活力的年轻人。这座雕像脸上的表情带有一种神秘的微笑。他英雄般的躯体青春永驻，散发出无限的美好、力量、希望与祝福。

The kouros is the most significant statuary type in Archaic art (7th-6th centuries B.C.) and embodies the aristocratic ideals of the era. He either depicts deities or mortal young men at the peak of their beauty and vigor. The expression on his face is characterized by an enigmatic smile. With his heroic nudity, he epitomizes perpetual youthfulness, eternal beauty, the power, hope and bliss of life.

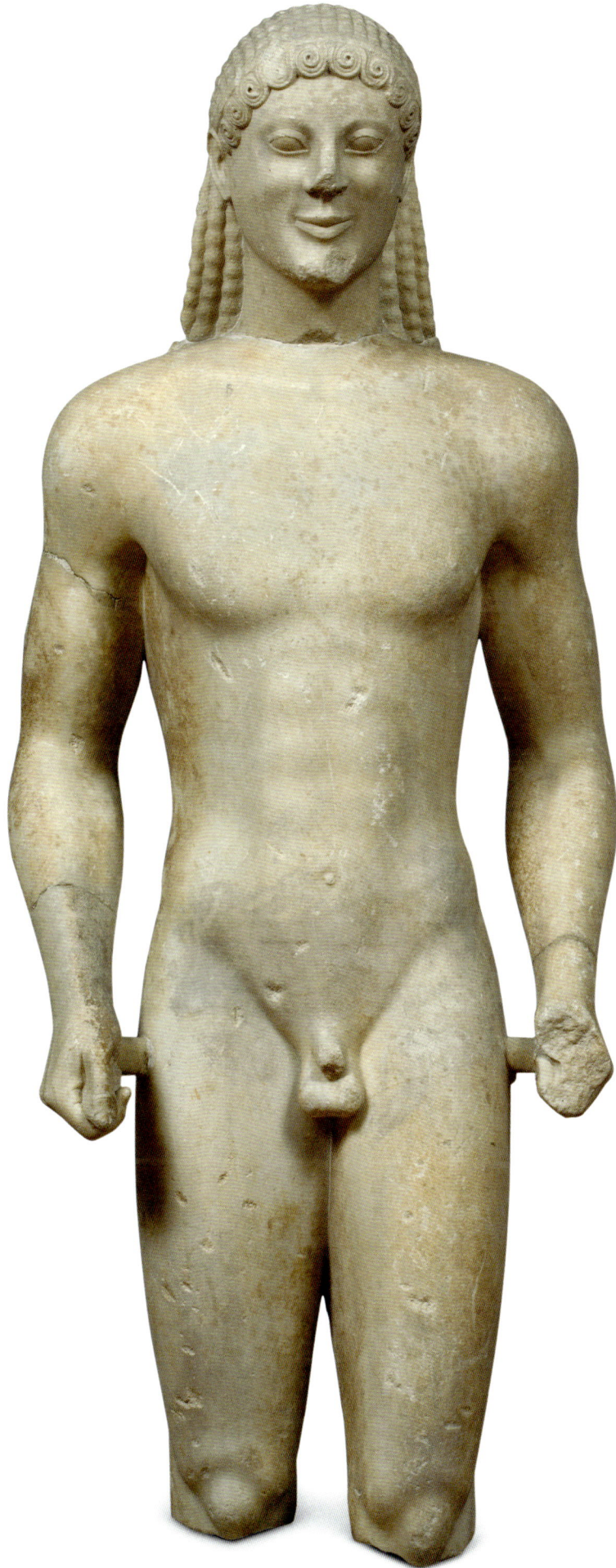

182

裸体男性躯干

来自雅典

公元前 5 世纪中叶青铜原作的罗马复制品

Nude male torso

From Athens

Roman recreation of a bronze original of the mid-5th century B.C.

HNAM Γ 1665

这座裸体雕像以强壮的四肢和线条分明的肌肉塑造了一个英雄般的男性形象。其很可能表现的是阿提卡的一位名祖英雄——安提奥库斯。

The volumes of the limbs and the musculature of the body of the male figure depicted in heroic nudity are rendered with a particular plasticity. Most probably a hero of Attica is represented, maybe the eponym hero Antiochus.

183

大理石男性躯干雕像

来自阿提卡地区的达夫尼

公元前 490 — 前 480 年

Marble torso of a male figure

From Daphni, Attica

490 – 480 B.C.

HNAM Γ 1605

这个充满力量的形象被解读为一名落于下风却仍殊死自卫的勇士。他的身体倒向现已遗失的左腿，同时他尽力将上半身转向相反的方向，充血膨胀的肌肉强调了四肢伸展的力度。仿佛可以看到这名勇士跪在地上，把头转向右上方，正举起右手全力反击。这座雕塑属于一组表现交战双方的群像。

The strongly moving figure is interpreted as a warrior, who, though defeated, keeps defending himself. The body is falling towards the lost left leg, while turning and strongly bending the upper part of the torso to the opposite direction. The accentuated plasticity of the musculature shows the intensity of the stretching of the limbs. The figure kneeling on the ground, turned the head to the right and upwards and raised the right hand to fight back. The sculpture belonged to a group along with the opponent.

184

束发带的青年雕像

来自基克拉迪群岛，提洛岛

公元前 100 年的作品，原件是公元前 440 — 前 420 年波利克里托斯的著名作品

这件作品是基于原作的一件现代复制品

Statue of a youth binding his hair (Diadoumenos)

From Delos, Cycldes

Work of 100 B.C. after a famous original of Polycleitus dating to 440 – 420 B.C.

The exhibit is a modern exact cast of the original work

HNAM Γ 1826

这座雕像表现了一个获得胜利的运动员，他完美的身体结构比肩神明，甚至可谓运动精神的理想化身。波利克里托斯将对称性原则和裸体男性身体的完美比例运用到雕塑中，他在《法则》一书中曾对此进行论述。

The statue represents a victorious athlete with divine features or even the embodiment itself of the athletic ideal. The sculptor has applied to it the principles of symmetry and the proportions of the nude male body that he discussed in his treatise *Canon*.

185

阿尔勒式阿佛洛狄忒大理石雕像的躯干部位

来自雅典昌西克拉特斯纪念亭区域

公元前 1 世纪对普拉克西特列斯的《狄斯比斯的阿佛洛狄忒》

（创作于公元前 370 — 前 360 年）的仿作

Marble torso of a statue of Aphrodite in the Arles type

From the area of Lysicrates Monument in Athens

1st century B.C.

Copy of the "Aphrodite of Thespies" by Praxiteles (370 – 360 B.C.)

HNAM Γ 227

　　女神半裸身体，手臂上戴着手镯，她看着左手中的镜子，同时伸出右手指向著名"交际花"芙里尼的雕像。其平滑的肌肤和柔软、富有弹性的肌肤渲染，强调了这座雕像的女性特质。

　　The goddess was depicted semi-nude, with a bracelet around the arm, looking at the mirror that she held in the left hand, while she stretched the right hand towards the statue of the famous courtesan Phryne. The smooth skin and the soft, sensual rendering of the flesh emphasize the femininity of the figure.

186

大理石阿佛洛狄忒头像

来自雅典的古罗马市集

公元前 4 世纪原作的罗马复制品

Marble head of Aphrodite

From the Roman Agora, Athens

Roman copy of a 4th-century B.C. original

HNAM Γ 1762

　　这座硕大的头像因其美貌而令人感到惊艳，她有着娇嫩的嘴唇、丰满的面颊、细长的凤眼和被弯曲的鬈发环绕的光洁额头。此头像来自一座经典的阿佛洛狄忒雕像，属于阿斯普雷蒙-林登/阿尔勒式类型。它复制了著名古典雕塑家普拉克西特列斯的原作，原作的模特是艺术家的伴侣、著名的"交际花"芙里尼。此头像的额头和下巴在基督教时代被刻上了十字架。

　　The remarkably beautiful colossal head is distinguished by the fleshy lips, full cheeks, narrow elongated eyes and triangular forehead, framed by wavy curls. It belongs to a classicizing statue of Aphrodite in the Aspremont-Lynden/Arles type that copies an original of the famous Classical sculptor Praxiteles. Praxiteles' model for depicting Aphrodite's divine beauty was his companion and famed courtesan, Phryne. The crosses on the forehead and chin of the figure were incised in the Christian era.

187

大理石男孩与鹅雕像

来自中希腊莉莱亚市的一处圣地

公元前 3 世纪

Marble statue of a boy with a goose

From a sanctuary in the city of Lilaia, Central Greece

3rd century B.C.

HNAM Γ 2772

　　一个胖乎乎、赤裸、微笑着的男孩正用左手按住停在一根低矮柱子上的鹅。他的右手抱着他心爱的玩具——一块羊拐。男孩的头饰可能暗示他正在参加某个庆典或仪式，甚至可能暗示他本身就是治疗儿科病的医神伊安尼斯科斯（医神阿斯克勒庇俄斯之子）。

　　A chubby, nude, smiling boy restrains his companion goose atop a low pillar with his open left palm. In his right hand he is holding to his chest his prized plaything, a knucklebone. The diadem that the boy wears on his head probably indicates participation in a festival or ritual or even his identification with Ianiskos, the divine boy-healer.

188

大理石年轻运动员雕像

来自阿提卡地区的厄琉息斯

公元前 2 世纪晚期（公元前 440 年原作的复制品）

Marble statue of a young athlete

From Eleusis, Attica

Late 2nd century B.C. (copy of an original of 440 B.C.)

HNAM Γ 254

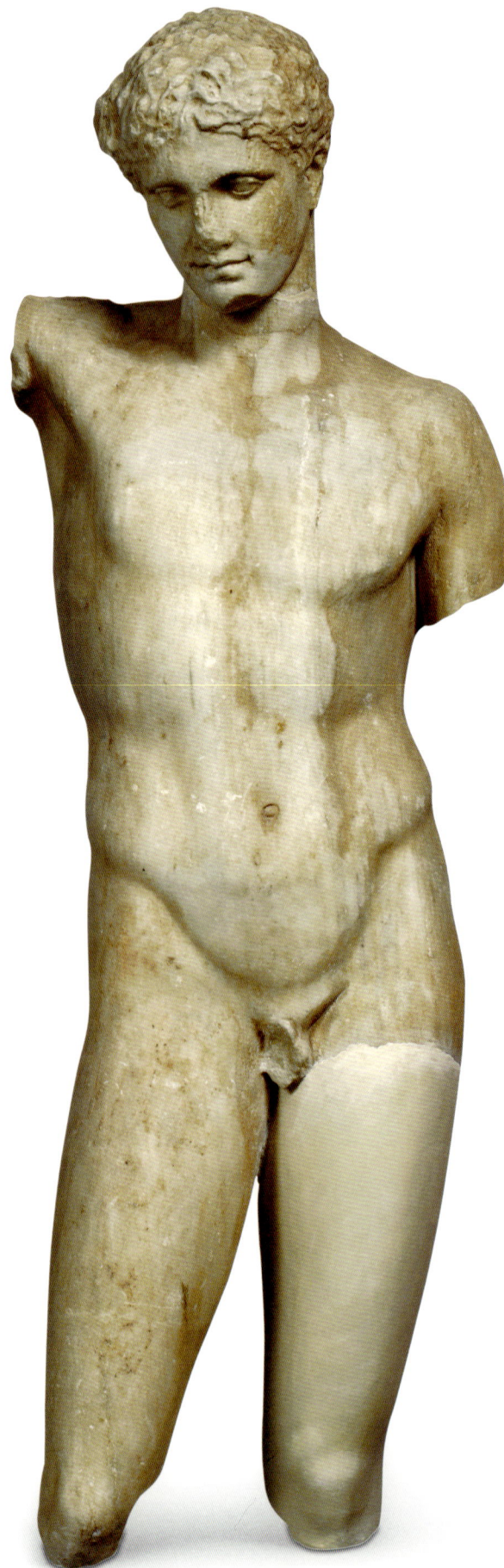

　　这座雕像和谐而有力地展现了年轻运动员身体的结构细节。这座雕像是对某件古典雕塑的复制或自发再创作，其原型很可能是由著名雕塑家波利克里托斯创作的运动员基尼斯科斯的雕像。

The anatomical details of the young athlete's body are rendered harmoniously and vigorously. The statue is a copy or a free reworking of a Classical sculpture, most probably a statue of the athlete Kyniskos, made by the famous sculptor Polykleitos.

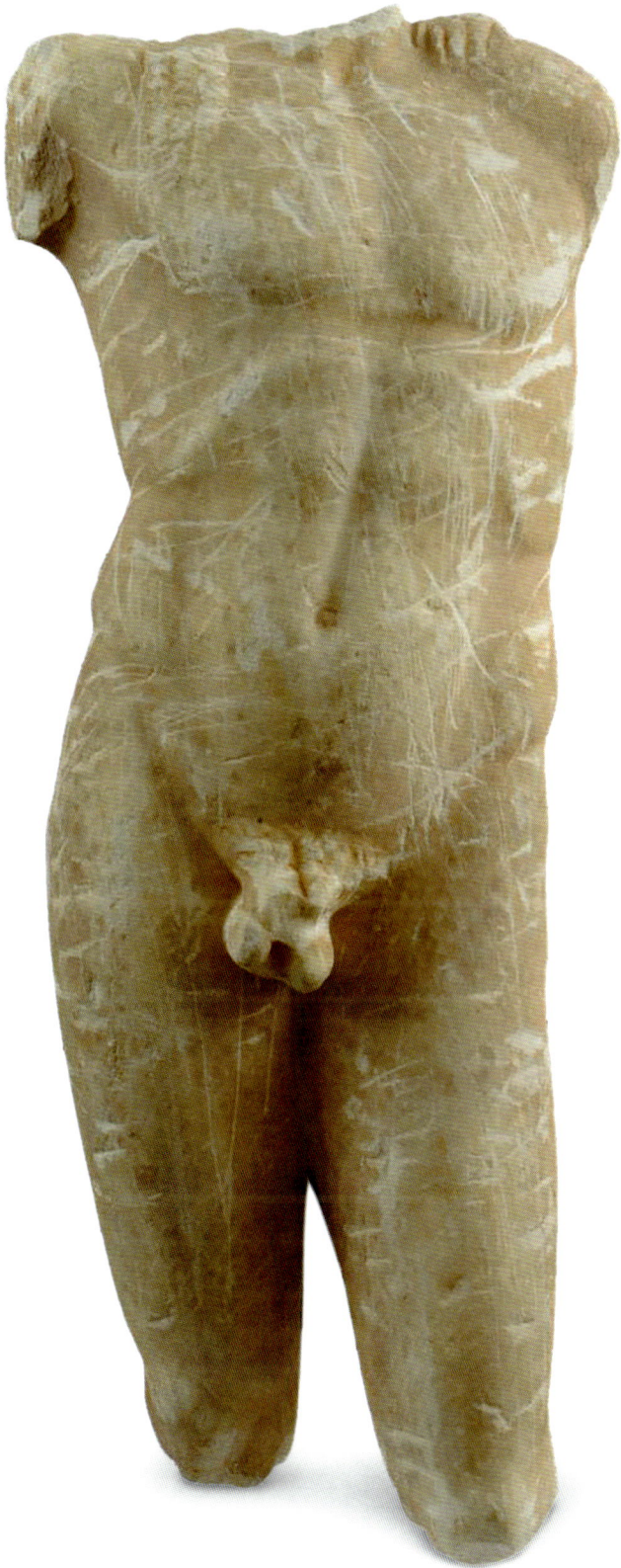

189

大理石萨提尔小雕像

来源未知，由卡拉帕诺斯收藏捐赠

公元前 2 世纪

Marble statuette of a Satyr

Unknown provenance. Donation by the Karapanos
Collection

2nd century B.C.

HNAM Γ 4800

　　这件作品是一组年轻的萨提尔和幼童雕像中的一部分，从山和森林之灵萨提尔左肩上的小手可以看出，原雕像的造型可能是他肩负着一名幼童。这座雕塑的表现手法和姿势明显受到了古典时期、波利克里托斯风格或普拉克西特列斯风格的影响。

The statuette is part of a group of a young Satyr and a child, which he was carrying, as indicated by its hand on the left shoulder of the Satyr. The sculptural rendering and the posture indicate influence by Classical, Polykleiteian or Praxiteleian prototypes.

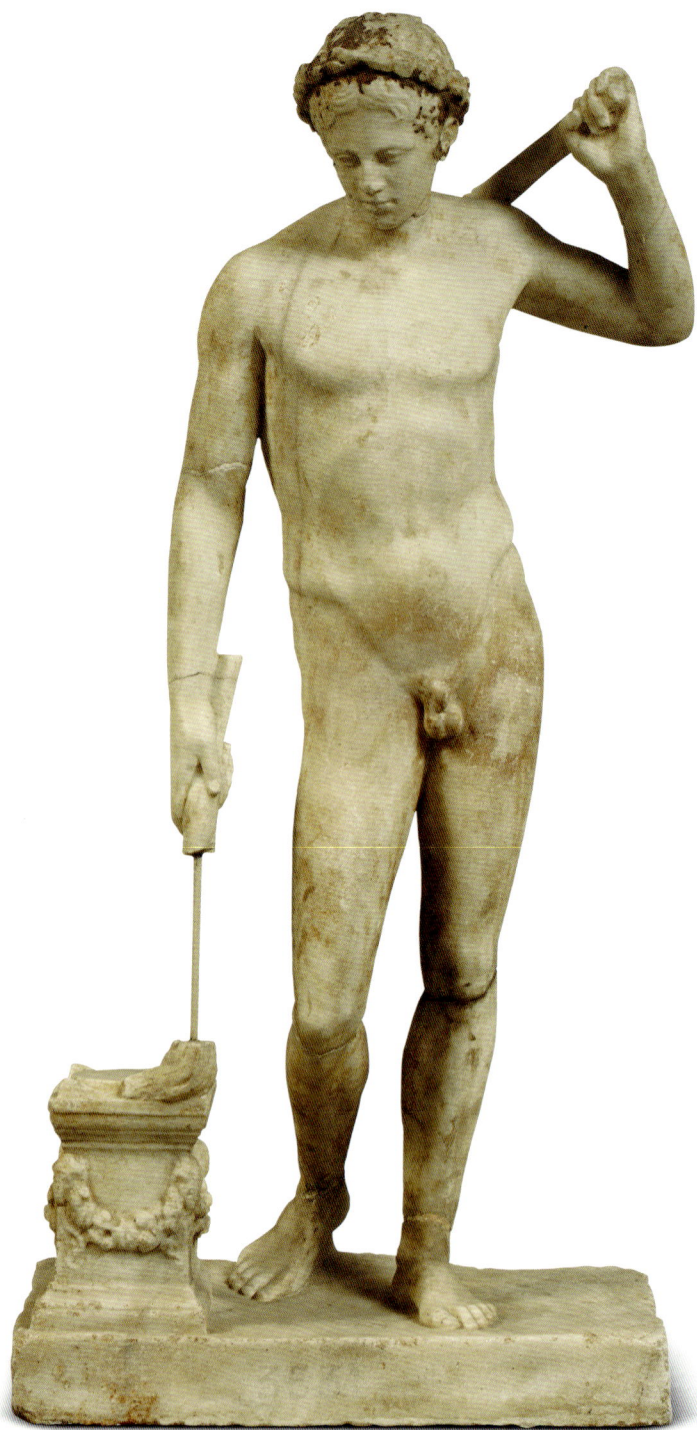

190

裸体青年大理石小雕像

来源未知，1927 年没收于伦敦

公元前 1 世纪晚期

Marble statuette of a nude youth

Unknown provenance, confiscated in London in 1927

Late 1st century B.C.

HNAM Γ 3631

　　这座小雕像是双人组雕之一的变体，该组雕分别被解释为俄瑞斯忒斯和皮拉德斯，或睡神修普诺斯和死神塔纳托斯。这座雕像被认为是死神的化身，因为他拿着一个倒转的火把指向祭坛，两者都是丧葬的象征。这座雕像的造型让人联想起经后世修改的公元前5世纪著名雕塑家波利克里托斯的雕像作品。

　　The statuette is a variation of one of the two figures of a group, which has been interpreted either as Orestes and Pylades, or as Hypnos (Sleep) and Thanatos (Death). The view that the figure is the personification of death is reinforced by the fact that he is holding a down-turned torch to an altar, both funerary symbols. The modelling of the figure recalls statues of the famous the 5th century B.C. sculptor, Polykleitus, modified in later times.

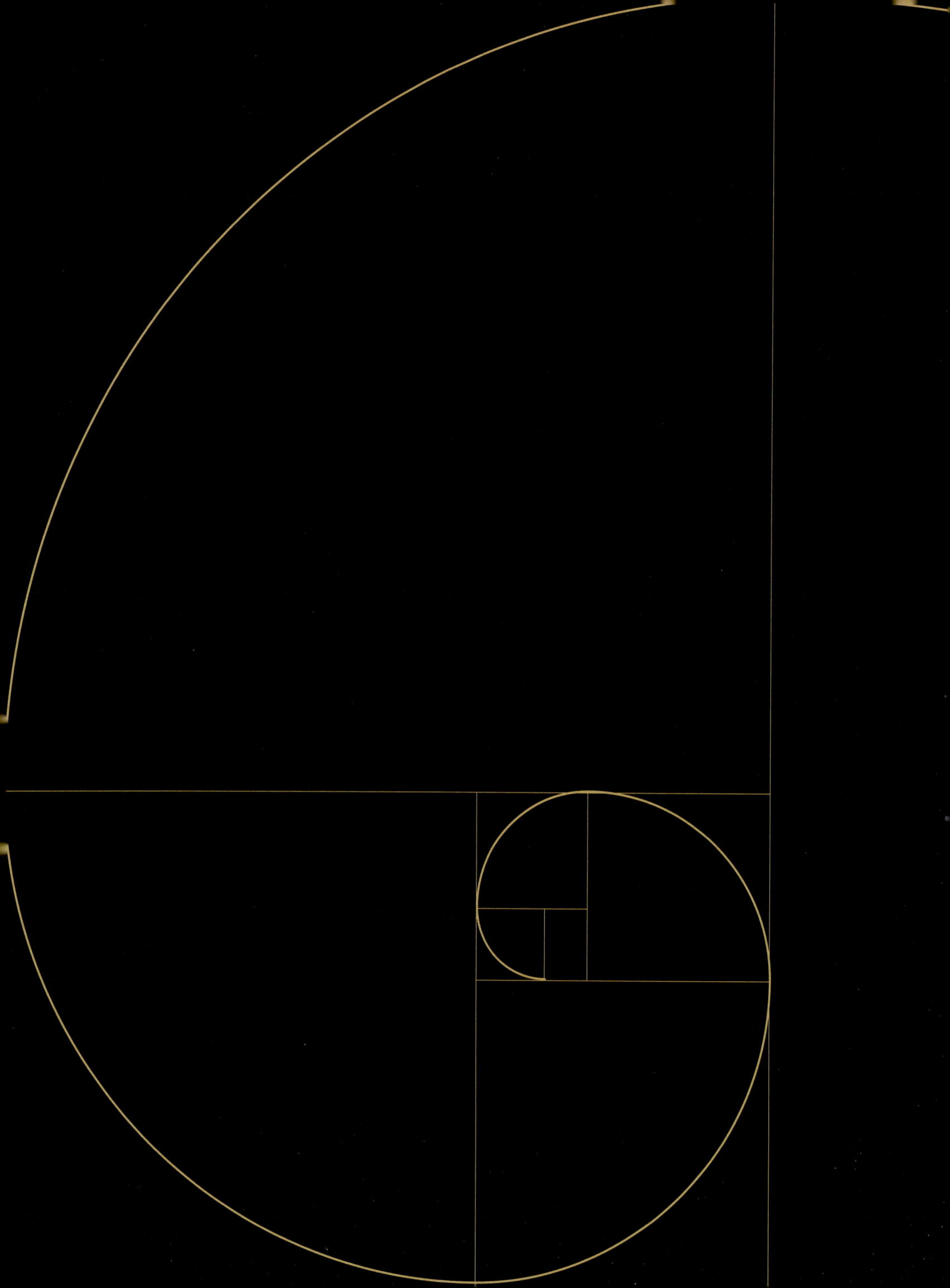

尾声：
美，无尽的求索

EPILOGUE:
ENDLESS QUEST

　　"美是什么？"这个由苏格拉底提出的问题一直牵动着古代哲学家、数学家、诗人和艺术家的思绪。探求仍在继续，答案无法一目了然。

　　纵观古希腊艺术的演变，我们可以感受到，对美的追求，即使最终无法导向绝对真理，也能引导我们认识自己的内心。千姿百态的美让我们对内心世界有了多层面的理解，也让我们距离人类的本性更进一步。

The question of Socrates "What is Beauty?" has engaged the thought of philosophers, mathematicians, poets and artists of Antiquity. The quest is continuing and has no easy or clear-cut answers.

When looking at the evolution of ancient Greek art, one can perceive that the pursuit of beauty, even if it does not end up to an absolute truth, can lead to acknowledging our inner self. The countless aspects of beauty offer a multifaceted understanding of our inner world and a more profound access to human nature.

191

大理石男子肖像头部

来自雅典

公元前 1 世纪

Marble male portrait head

From Athens

1st century B.C.

HNAM Γ 320

这是一个无名人物的真实面孔，承载着短暂的思绪和日常的烦忧。其额头和眼角的皱纹以及忧郁的表情，都无不与古典美学的理想范式形成鲜明对比。

A realistic face of an anonymous figure carrying the burden of ephemeral thoughts and everyday concerns. The wrinkles on the forehead and at the edges of the eyes, along with the melancholic expression, are characteristics that contrast the idealism of the classic rule.